TOM
DALEY

TOM
DALEY

The Unauthorized Biography

Chas Newkey-Burden

Michael O'Mara Books Limited

First published in Great Britain in 2011 by
Michael O'Mara Books Limited
9 Lion Yard
Tremadoc Road
London SW4 7NQ

A CIP catalogue record for this book is available from the
British Library.

Papers used by Michael O'Mara Books Limited are natural,
recyclable products made from wood grown in sustainable forests.
The manufacturing processes conform to the environmental
regulations of the country of origin.

ISBN: 978-1-84317-608-4 in hardback print format
ISBN: 978-1-84317-769-2 in EPub format
ISBN: 978-1-84317-770-8 in Mobipocket format

1 2 3 4 5 6 7 8 9 10

Cover design by
Designed and typ
Printed and bour   ) 4YY
www.mombooks

Dedicated with love and gratitude to my three
champion nieces: Rose, May and Verity.
How fearless and fun you were as we sped
down the waterslides at Windsor Leisure Centre.

CONTENTS

INTRODUCTION

WHEN EXPERIENCED diving coach Andy Banks first watched Tom Daley in action at his local pool, his expert verdict was instant and clear-cut: 'I don't think he'll ever make it as a diver,' said Banks as he saw Tom trembling with nerves. 'He's not got a prayer.' Nearly ten years later, Tom is a world champion and double-Commonwealth gold-winning diving sensation. He is also Britain's greatest hope for the 2012 Olympics in London. What's more, the man who guided him to all this success is none other than Andy Banks. What a turn of fortunes for the once nervous youngster from Devon.

Tom has described himself as 'normal, but not quite normal because of all the diving stuff'. In truth, he has always been anything other than normal. Most children, when they are nine years old, dream of becoming an astronaut, a footballer, a pop star or a vet. Others do not have a clue what they want to do when they are older, they are too busy simply being kids and living in the moment. Tom's dream has long been clear in his mind. As a nine-year-old boy he drew a picture of himself, upside-down on a diving board, with the Olympic logo next to him and London 2012 emblazoned above him. On his face in the drawing Tom wore a triumphant smile. The sketch was topped-off with a written caption: 'My ambition.'

The fertile imagination of youth does not get much more specific than that. 'It's just everyone's dream when they are a little kid,' he said. 'Everyone wants to be an Olympian and get an Olympic gold medal.' Well, it certainly was *his* dream – and it is one he is in a good position to fulfil. In the summer of 2012, the hopes of the nation and the eyes of the world will all be on this young man from Plymouth, as he takes a deep breath and leaps off the board at the Aquatics Centre in the Olympic Park, plunging at thirty miles an hour into the water and towards destiny.

Tom describes diving as 'controlled falling'. What would drive somebody to take up such a sport? The risks are obvious. On two occasions Tom has smashed his head against the board on his way down, blood pouring out by the time he hit the water. However, he is full of determination, so he was soon back on the board, working and honing his skill, resolved to be the best. He trains six days a week for a minimum of four hours each time. The preparation is psychological as well as physical. Tom says he has taught himself to have a 'sat-nav' in his head, to help him perfect the intricate movements his dives contain. When a dive works for him, the rush of adrenaline he gets is, he says, unbeatable.

As he has reached the top of his game, he has built a fond fan-base and gained a high media presence. Tom has been interviewed and profiled by the world's media countless times. He has won three BBC Young Sports Personality of the Year awards and presented a BAFTA. He has been photographed alongside Kate Moss for *Vogue*, the magazine that describes Tom as 'one of the people that will define the decade'.

The media loves Tom, and Tom – who dreams of becoming a television presenter once he stops diving – loves it back. One of his former synchro partners witnessed first hand the press's fascination with Tom. 'I felt as if I didn't matter,' Blake Aldridge told me. 'We would win a medal together and all the headlines would be about Tom. My name would just be in small print. We had our photograph taken together on the rostrum with our gold medals, but the media cropped me out. I didn't blame Tom, but it was demoralizing.'

Away from the boards, Tom has had bitter challenges of his own. His father Rob spent the last five years of his life battling brain cancer. Tom's relationship with his father was immensely close and intense, so Rob's long illness and subsequent tragic death in May

2011 has been particularly hard for his son to come to terms with. Meanwhile, in his still brief life, Tom has had his own demons to face in the form of bullying that he suffered at school after he took part in his first Olympics tournament at fourteen. Bullying that became so bad that Tom changed schools.

Yet somehow he has kept his focus on diving. He became a world champion even as he faced these horrors. He has the 'whole package' needed to become a serious sporting idol: good looks, down-to-earth charm and success. As such, his narrative is simply irresistible: destiny links him with London 2012. He will turn eighteen just before the tournament begins. 'He was born at the right time, learnt to swim at the right time,' said Rob. 'We've got a great facility five minutes from our home, the London Olympics was unveiled at the right time. It's all there for him.'

CHAPTER ONE

•

A Pilgrim is Born

'The thing that makes Tom and the great ones so great is that they just seem to be born with it.'
STEVE FOLEY, national performance director of British Diving and former Olympic diver

TOM WAS FIRST SET ON THE PATH to diving by his father – but only inadvertently so. Rob Daley decided to make sure his first-born son learned to swim as early as possible in life, not because he saw a path to sporting success, but simply because he wanted to make sure Tom would be safe as he grew up. The Daleys live in Plymouth, and in that Devonian seaside city one is never far from water. This suited Tom from the start: his first trip to the pool and then the local beach came when he was just four months old. 'Anything like that he absolutely loved,' recalled his mother, Debbie. After hearing several tragic stories of local drowning accidents, Tom's parents decided to take their son to learn to swim at the local pool when he was still just three years of age. 'There was nothing competitive about it at the start,' said the protective father. 'It was about survival, not showing off. We live by the sea. I wanted him to know how to handle himself.' Sensible thinking, and little could Rob have known what a fateful day that was to be for his son.

After all, the Daleys have never been a family that actively sought out particular greatness. The only hint in Tom's heritage that he might be destined for the diving board lies in the fact that when Rob was a child he had enjoyed the odd bit of leaping of a different kind. 'When I was a kid I liked jumping off rocks and cliffs,' Rob once wrote. But although Rob enjoyed the adrenaline of that activity, he soon grew out of it.

The Daleys are a decent, regular Devon family. Debbie told the *Observer* that nowadays she expects people assume her family is 'stuck-up, or rich to the back teeth', but they are not. 'When people meet us they say, "You're just like everybody, you're a normal Plymouth family,"' she said. 'And we are.'

Thomas Robert Daley was born on 21 May 1994. His parents were absolutely delighted with their first child. They were both fairly young when Tom came along, Rob was twenty-four, Debbie was twenty-three. Rob, a former taxi driver, ran his own business, a company that designed and built machinery, while Debbie worked part-time as a financial administrator in a nursery. Two years later, a second son – William – came along. Three years after that came Ben. By this stage, after his early introduction to the sport, the eldest of the three boys had already developed a love of swimming.

The year of Tom's birth proved to be an eventful one. In Britain, the National Lottery was launched, future Prime Minister Tony Blair was chosen as the new, young, leader of the Labour Party, and changes in the trading laws meant that shops were allowed to open on a Sunday for the first time. In the wider world, Nelson Mandela became the first black leader of South Africa, an earthquake hit Los Angeles, killing twenty people, and pop star Michael Jackson married Lisa Marie, the daughter of rock 'n' roll legend Elvis Presley.

Back home in Plymouth, the young toddler had more pressing matters on his mind. 'Tom used to be afraid of Mister Blobby,' said Debbie of the early years of one of Plymouth's most courageous sporting sons. Indeed, it is a measure of his importance that not yet out of his teens he is already one of the more famous people to come from the Devonian city. Quite rightly, the people of Plymouth are extremely proud of Tom's achievements. 'It's so important to recognize Tom's achievement as a city,' said Vivien Pengelly, then leader of Plymouth City Council. 'He's a world champion and to have a world champion who comes from Plymouth is absolutely fantastic.'

Tom adores his city and is proud of it. 'I love the way it is right in the centre of Devon and Cornwall,' he wrote. 'Rugged beauty can be found just behind us in Dartmoor.' Other well-known 'Plymouthians' include Sir Francis Drake (the first Englishman to circumnavigate the globe) and explorer Robert Falcon Scott (better known as Scott of the Antarctic). Indeed, Drake once famously finished a game of bowls on Plymouth Hoe, before taking on and beating the Spanish Armada.

Plymouth is one Devon's best-known and loved cities. It is a lively, waterfront area of land, with beautiful English countryside never far away. National Trust buildings abound. A place of maritime heritage steeped in history, its Barbican port is where the *Mayflower* left for its voyage to the New World. Among the city's many aquatic attractions are the National Marine Aquarium, where the popular Atlantic Ocean tank proudly displays the best collection of sharks and rays in Europe. Then there is a popular refurbished art-deco lido and Plymouth Sound, a bay that is popular among fans of water sports. 'Awesome' is how Tom describes the lido. Among those water sports enthusiastically pursued by Plymouthians and visitors alike are yacht and dingy sailing, canoeing, surfing and jet skiing. As we shall see, Tom has become a keen jet-skier in recent times. Cut into the rocks at Tinside Lido are outdoor swimming pools, filled with seawater. The bay is also the site of much iconic photography and footage of The Beatles, who visited the area while filming their movie *Magical Mystery Tour*. The annual Port of Plymouth Regatta is one of the oldest such events in the world, and has been a regular feature of local life since 1823.

Tom is now a spokesman for the area. In 2011, the Plymouth Tourist Board issued a new brochure detailing the delights of the city, the introduction to which was written by Tom. 'There is positively nowhere like Plymouth,' he began, going on to describe the city as a 'water-sports haven'. He also highlighted his love of 'walking and exploring the Barbican harbour front; the cobbled streets and historic architecture.' Internationally famous sailor Pete Goss and broadcaster Angela Rippon also provided written contributions to the brochure, but it was Tom that took top billing. He was a poster boy for Plymouth long before he began to become one for the whole of Britain.

Sports-wise, the city is not among the greats of the big games. Plymouth Argyle is the local football team, which has had some notable players on its books, including goalkeeping legends Bruce Grobbelaar and Peter Shilton. Nicknamed 'The Pilgrims', the club has never troubled the upper reaches of the footballing tree. Although his father was a keen supporter, Tom is not a fan of them, or any other football team, but he does go and watch Argyle play occasionally. His brothers prefer to look eastwards and up to London when it comes to football – both are ardent Chelsea fans.

Other local sporting institutions include Plymouth Albion rugby union club and the Plymouth Raiders basketball side. There are a fair number of smaller clubs and teams in the city across various sports and games, however, it's reasonable to say that Plymouth is a city that had long been crying out for a real sporting legend in its midst. Little wonder then that it's so thrilled with Tom's diving successes.

For those who believe in astrology, Tom is a Gemini. People born under this sign are renowned for being chatty, full of energy and life, and Geminis are also said to be intensely curious people. Famous Geminis include actors Johnny Depp and Marilyn Monroe, tennis star Venus Williams, singers Paul McCartney and Lenny Kravitz. Tom was born on the first day of the Gemini sign, so is therefore considered 'on the cusp' with the previous sign of the cycle – Taurus. Astrologers believe that Taurus folk are dependable, stable types. Famous Taurus folk include football star David Beckham, actor Al Pacino and singer/actress Barbra Streisand. As we shall see, Tom does indeed represent a hybrid of the lively Gemini and the more patient steadiness of a Taurean.

Less contested than astrology is the effect that the order in which a person is born in their family has on their personality. More and more studies suggest that the fact that someone is the youngest, eldest or middle child in the family has a notable bearing on their personality. At a basic level, this stands to reason: the formative years are generally considered to be the first seven or eight years of one's life. That is a time in which your place in the family is pivotal to your experience and existence.

As the eldest of the Daley offspring, according to birth order theory Tom is expected to have a nurturing, organized and caring nature. 'I actually get along with my youngest brother best,' said Tom during a web-chat with his fans in 2011. 'I also get along with William really well,' he added, but it is with Ben that Tom has the strongest bond. This side of his character has become increasingly important as his life has progressed, and never was it more important than when his father's illness threw the family into a state of shock and fear in 2006, when his younger brothers needed a caring and loving elder sibling to look after them.

Other factors that are common to first-born children are a superior ability to communicate. This derives from the fact that they will have spent more time during their formative years listening to adults converse and interact with one another than would siblings born subsequently. Tom has obviously seen the benefits of this. From an early age he was a polished media performer who spoke fluently during television and radio interviews despite minimal media training. This is in contrast to his brothers, who, during a 2010 BBC documentary made about Tom and his family, were uneasy in front of camera – as a lot of kids would be. Tom's linguistic and communicative grace can also be seen in his willingness to study other languages at school and college, including Spanish, which is one of his favourite languages. (He also chose to learn it because many diving competitions are held in Mexico.) Tom is a well-mannered and kind boy, both qualities installed in him by Rob and Debbie. 'We've always taught him to be polite,' said Rob.

•

While Tom was growing from a baby to a toddler to a child in Devon, events elsewhere in the world were already shaping his future as an Olympic diver. For instance, when Tom was just four years of age, a diver from Quebec in Canada first came to widespread public attention. He was in due course to become Tom's hero, the athlete who continues to inspire him to this day. Alexandre Despatie began diving at the age of five, in the pool in the back garden of his family home. At the 1998 Commonwealth Games, which were held in Kuala Lumpur, Malaysia, Despatie performed with astonishing heroism. He was just thirteen years of age and yet he won a gold medal on the 10-metre diving platform. Remarkable. Not only that, his victory was achieved with perfect 10 score-lines. To add to his glory, Despatie became the youngest gold medal winner in the history of the Commonwealth Games, and was therefore included in the 2000 edition of the *Guinness Book of World Records*. Tom explained that Despatie is his role model, 'because he is the youngest ever Commonwealth Games champion in diving'.

The first Olympic Games tournament during Tom's life was held in 1996 in Atlanta, Georgia in the United States. Tom was just two years old, so was unaware of the competitiveness and excitement that unfolded there, after US President Bill Clinton and boxing legend Muhammad Ali had opened proceedings. However, the English city of Manchester had bid to host that tournament and though it had not succeeded in its bid, it seemed that the games were edging their way ever closer to Britain. Manchester again bid to host the 2000 Olympics and came closer – but not close enough – to winning the bid, which was instead sealed by Sydney, Australia.

By 2004, the year of the Athens Olympics, Tom was firmly in the diving community. When the Beijing

Olympics came round in 2008, Tom was ready to take part, and by the time that tournament was held, London had already won in its bid to hold the 2012 games.

From the moment it was revealed in July 2005 that the London bid had been successful, it seemed destined that Tom would thrive during it. Some of the people he finds most inspiring are figures from past Olympic Games. 'There have been lots of inspirational people in my life,' said Tom. 'People like the Olympic greats Sir Steve Redgrave, Dame Tanni Grey-Thompson. Olympic heroes.'

He has also spoken with fondness of decathlete Daley Thompson, and not just because 'he shares my name'. These are the sorts of sporting icons he has, and will continue to try to emulate in his own career – aims he is in with a shout of realizing if he continues to focus on his sport as fiercely as he has thus far. His father, Rob, also had many Olympic heroes. He continued to measure Tom against them. 'When you think of the Olympics you think of names like Steve Redgrave, Seb Coe and Linford Christie,' said Rob.

'They're absolutely the Olympic icons, aren't they?' enthused Tom. 'The best ever. It's like "wow", that's what you'd love to be able to do in the Olympics.' Who would bet against him?

First, though, he had to develop that interest in swimming. It was only by regularly visiting swimming pools in Plymouth that Tom's gaze wandered towards the diving boards that would, literally, propel him to fame. He had learned to swim early in life and by the age of four Tom was already pretty confident in the water. He was certainly a more accomplished swimmer than most kids his age. This was not just childish splashing around – although Tom made sure he had lots of fun among the serious stuff. He was, without doubt, a real natural, quickly attaining his 2,000-metre distance badge and showed great aptitude in the pool. He was obviously enjoying himself, too. However, it was a few years before he would move on to diving.

Looking back, he is keen to play down his early years in the pool: 'I was just a regular swimmer,' he said. 'My dad thought it was a great idea, because we live by the sea, to learn to swim, just in case you get into any trouble.' But how could Rob have known that by encouraging Tom to learn to swim so early he was setting in motion a chain of events that would make his son a world-renowned athlete? For, as he splashed around in the local baths, Tom's gaze kept turning towards those diving boards at the end of the pool. That looks fun, he thought . . .

CHAPTER TWO

●

Dive In!

'Probably the best £25 I ever spent.'
DEBBIE DALEY

AS THEY GROW UP most British boys, if they are
interested in sport at all, are most likely to be interested
in football. Not Tom, who quickly fell for the charms of
diving. 'I found it came naturally and was much more
enjoyable than playing football,' said Tom of his early
experiences. It is a fairly surprising fact that although
Tom is a successful sportsman, with an undeniably
athletic physique, he is not one of those athletes who
loves and successfully masters every sport he turns his
hand to. Indeed, there are some sports he is not keen on
at all. 'I did try football at school but I could never kick a
ball in a straight line,' he said. 'I'm not very coordinated
with that kind of stuff.' In 2008 there were reports that
Tom was on the brink of signing a million-pound
contract to be mentored by football superstar David

Beckham, but nothing ever came of the rumour, other than a firm denial of it by Rob: 'absolute rubbish'.

Among the non-aquatic sports in which he has taken an interest are judo, squash and tennis. In judo he enjoyed some success, reaching the orange-belt level and winning some junior trophies. However, it was diving that really captured his imagination. Tom was seven when he started diving, after concluding that it looked 'more exciting' to dive than to swim.

'I saw the people diving off the boards and I thought I'd give it a go, and did Saturday morning lessons. While all the other people were mucking around and not listening, I really enjoyed it and wanted to get better and better,' he said. 'So my dad took me along regularly on Saturday mornings and after a while I got talent spotted. It's amazing I just got picked out of nowhere.'

During those Saturday morning sessions, Tom liked what he experienced. 'As soon as I started diving, I knew it was for me. It's like being on a rollercoaster, the loop-the-loops and everything like that. It has the adrenalinee rush of a rollercoaster every time.'

His newfound love was shared by his brother William, who became interested in diving around the same time. However, William was to lose interest as Tom's success in the sport soared. 'I started diving at the same time as Tom,' William said. 'Then I got a higher grade than him so I moved on to a higher level. Then I was better than him, but when I was down my caravan I kind of did a back dive off the pool and then hit my legs at the side of the pool . . . So then I stopped doing it.'

Instead, Tom's brother became more interested in football and, particularly, rugby. Asked if he has ever wished that he had in fact kept going, William said: 'All my mates tell me if I'd have kept going I could be as good as Tom, stuff like that.' We will never know how true this is. It was Tom who kept up with the diving, after his parents had paid £25 for a set of five lessons. 'Probably the best £25 I ever spent,' said Debbie.

Tom is not the only Englishman to start diving at an early age and take it up as a serious sport. Actor Jason Statham spent twelve years diving with the national squad, and for a while in the early 1990s he was ranked twelfth in the world. He had been inspired to take up the sport after falling under the spell of the James Bond-like character in the television advertisements for Milk Tray chocolates. When they were shown on the television, the all-action character featured in the advert became the hero of many a young lad. After stealthily delivering chocolate to a lady in the dead of night, our hero is seen running to a cliff, off which he dives heroically.

A more recent British diving star is Tom's sometime

synchro partner Peter Waterfield, who has tasted success as a solo diver, and in synchronized events with his former dive partner Leon Taylor. Waterfield won gold at the 2002 Commonwealth Games in Manchester, and silver at the Olympics in Athens two years later. His most successful dive partner, Taylor, was hyperactive as a child and his parents funnelled his energies into sport in the hope it would help him displace his energy in a positive way. Taylor speaks positively of his experiences in the game, which, he said, gave him some wonderful times and helped shape him as a character. 'It was a great experience, you know, to travel the world and compete at a certain level,' he said. 'It teaches you discipline, focus, and certainly keeps you out of trouble.'

All of these experiences and benefits were still to come for Tom when he started diving. It was at the Central Park leisure pool in Plymouth that he first learned to properly dive, with those £25 lessons. Standing on Mayflower Drive, it is a fairly unremarkable venue. The complex includes a learner pool, a six-lane swimming pool and a diving pool. It's not the world's greatest pool – it's not even Britain's greatest pool. It is, though, the place that one of Britain's finest sportsmen first learned his craft and is therefore of increasing national significance. Without it, everything in Tom's life would have been entirely different, and you would not now be reading this book. 'There's no doubt about it, if this facility wasn't here I wouldn't be a diver,' he said.

He was a little anxious when he first climbed the stairs to the first board at Central Park, but soon built up the confidence to dive. He actually found that diving gave him more courage and confidence in his life in general. 'Dive off there,' he said during a later interview, while pointing at the 10-metre board in Central Park, 'and you don't find much scary.' Indeed, so central in his life story is the venue that he has since returned to Central Park to be interviewed and photographed in the surroundings of where it all started. These media slots have focused attention on the place that it would not have otherwise received, and consequently the diving community has tried to use this focus as a springboard to improving the facilities there.

In truth, the venue is far from an ideal training centre for divers. 'They are really doing it the hard way in Plymouth, with a sub-standard facility,' said British Diving's national performance director Steve Foley. Although Plymouth is one of four high-performance centres in the United Kingdom, it was the only one without international standard boards available. This meant that athletes often had to travel to one of the other three high-performance centres to do part of their training. The nearest one was in Southampton, a drive of more than three hours away. Hardly ideal for anyone, least of all an athlete in training whose body can ill-afford seven-hour round trips just for a bit of training. Consequently, Tom's early days diving were all spent at Central Park.

By the time he celebrated his eighth birthday Tom was already showing very promising signs as a diver. He loved the challenges and the adrenaline rush that diving brought to his life. He felt alive as he flung himself off the board, heading for the cold splash of water as he landed. Not that this progress had come without a challenge. He later recalled the terror he felt when he first climbed up to the 10-metre board. 'I was terrified, walking to the edge I was nearly crawling, holding onto the railings and looking over and thinking "Oh my god, it's so high up here." It's terrifying, but once you've done it once, you want to do it again and again.'

Even after two years of diving, during which he honed and refined his technique and built on his ever-growing reserves of courage, there were still challenges to come for Tom. At the age of nine he faced a particularly harrowing prospect – his first backward dive. Here, he had to learn to detach himself from his fears and trust that he would complete the process safely. It was, literally and metaphorically, a case of 'taking the plunge'. To say that Tom felt uncertain as he prepared to try his first backward dive would be an understatement. The poor lad was reduced to tears.

As he recalled the moments leading up to the dive, he reconnected for a moment with the extreme trepidation he felt before finally going for it, and the immediate sense of relief and confidence he felt once he had. 'I stood on the platform crying my eyes out because I didn't want to perform a backward dive for the first time,' he said. 'When I finally plucked up enough courage to do it, I never looked back.' This single moment is crucial in Tom's life and career: as pivotal as the moment he had first decided to try diving, two years earlier. Had he not been able to find the courage to put aside his fears of the backward dive, he would not have progressed as a diver. In truth, he would probably have quickly lost interest in the sport all together. Diving would have defeated him, and the world might never have heard of this extraordinary young man.

Instead, though, he summoned up the courage and did the backward dive, and so entered a new phase in his life. From this point on he was on fire and indomitable, determined to continue working at his technique and really make something of his life. The adrenaline rush he had so enjoyed from previous dives was multiplied when he set off on a backward dive. Diving, he now felt increasingly sure, was his root to happiness and success.

It was his father Rob who usually took Tom to the pool to practice his diving. With his days of jumping off rocks long gone, Rob himself had never been a true diver, nor a particularly athletic person. Throughout his life he often suffered from motion sickness and was more than content to let Tom be the athletic member of the Daley clan. His feeling of destiny for Tom was immense from early on, and Tom repaid this faith by becoming a world champion and double-Commonwealth gold medal winner.

•

Diving as a sport has changed a lot during its history. The first known British Championships were held in Highgate in 1895, and in Scotland in 1889. At this time, the action became a 'dive' only at the moment the competitor hit the water, as opposed to now when it is what happens *before* that point that is considered crucial. In those days, the motion involved was less of a dive, more of a plunge. The highest point above water that participants dived from in those days was around six feet, somewhat less intimidating a prospect than the 10-metre height from which Tom and his fellow divers jump today. Within six years, however, things got tougher as people jumped from as high as 30 feet.

The evolution of the dive towards the more spectacular and intricate thing we know and love today was, in part, prompted by gymnasts rather than swimmers. In some European countries gymnasts preferred to practise their acrobatic jumps over water, rather than on a mat or on the floor, in order to ensure a smoother landing. So they would move their equipment and practise their mid-air twists and somersaults over water. This then developed into a sport of its own, that was for some time known as 'fancy diving' – a lovely, quaint term.

During the opening decades of the twentieth century, diving became more and more popular. Diving was first introduced as an Olympic sport during the 1904 Olympics. At first it was the Americans who were most successful in competition but the British soon began to catch up. In Britain, the 1920s saw the opening of the first diving club at Highgate in north London. Those who take part in diving today sometimes complain about the facilities in British pools and clubs, but back then, divers would have to climb up rusty ladders to reach the creaky and precarious boards. Then, as they prepared to jump, they would brace themselves for the muddy water, which sometimes contained litter. For many years the Highgate club was for men only. As diving grew in popularity, another club opened in Brockwell, in south-east London. Women's diving was included in the Olympic Games in 1912, and the first women's springboard competition took place in 1920. Then, in 1928, women took part in their first high-board diving competitions, and the sport became truly open for all.

The sport has its own language, and it is of advantage to the reader to understand some of the more common diving terms at this stage. The 'platform' is the solid, stationary structure from which divers launch themselves, whereas the 'springboard' is, as one might expect, a more 'springy' structure from which to jump. The 'synchronized' diving, or 'synchro', refers to when two divers of the same gender perform a simultaneous dive. Dives are assessed and marked by judges, who award scores between 0 and 10. However, dives are also assessed by the degree of difficulty – ranging from 1.2 to 4.2 – and a diver's final score for a dive is calculated by multiplying the degree of difficulty by the sum of the judges' scores. The key position in diving to understand at this stage is the 'pike', which is the position in which the knees are straight and the body is folded forward at the waist, with toes pointed.

●

As we have seen, when he was nine years old, Tom drew a picture in a scribbling book. A self-portrait, in it he is wearing red trunks and doing a handstand. On either side of him are the Olympic rings logo, and the words 'London 2012'. Above the picture, he had written in multi-coloured writing: 'My ambition.' There, on paper, was clearly spelt and drawn-out what Tom believed was his destiny. His family, too, shared his fateful feeling for 2012. 'The International Olympic Committee hadn't even chosen London back then, and I'd only been diving for a year, but I think it was a premonition,' said Tom. A confident premonition, but one not lacking justification, for by this stage Tom was already earmarked as a potentially huge prospect for the future. He had come under the eyes of a very skilled and impressive diving coach, who quickly shared Tom's confidence in his prospects.

But not *that* quickly: for the coach's first words on watching Tom at the pool were: 'I don't think he'll ever make it as a diver.'

CHAPTER THREE

•

'He's Not Got a Prayer'

'I miss out on things all the time because of training
– sometimes I get invited to barbecues or parties and
I can't go – but you have to make sacrifices . . . My
dream is to win gold in London 2012.'

TOM DALEY

IN THE STORY OF MANY successful people there is that
one fateful moment in which they are discovered by
the mentor who would expertly guide them to the top.
Sometimes, the narrative of such a discovery is smooth
and graceful. Other times it is a less than polished,
straightforward affair. This was the case with Tom's
discovery. As Plymouth-based diving coach Andy
Banks told the BBC, he was sitting at his desk one day
when someone phoned him and suggested he go to
the poolside, as a very special child had been spotted
diving. 'So I went over to the pool, sat down at the
side and watched him for twenty minutes,' recalled

Banks. 'At the end of the twenty minutes, I made the greatest comment ever: "I don't think he'll ever make it as a diver – he's not got a prayer."'

If you had told Banks there and then that Tom would not only become a diver, but that he would also become his client and that together they would make Tom a world champion, one of the most successful and famous divers of all time, he would not have believed you for a moment.

To be fair to Banks, based on the evidence available to him at the time, he had reached an understandable conclusion. 'In my defence, he didn't actually get in the pool,' continued Banks. 'He stood at the back of the first board, and cried for twenty minutes and refused to get on. He was very stubborn and there was no way he was doing anything. It was the attitude, more than anything else, that made me make the comment.'

It was the sports director of Plymouth Diving, Sam Grevett, who had first notified Banks about Tom. 'I spoke to . . . Andy Banks and told him I had a kid who was really good,' said Grevett. 'The coach came over and watched for ten minutes. After just ten minutes he said he would never make a diver as he's not got the bottle – he said Tom was too scared.'

Once he finally saw Tom dive, though, something Banks saw in him made the coach persevere. To try and build the youngster's confidence, Banks adopted a novel but effective technique by invoking a literary hero, familiar to most young people – and certainly to Tom. 'The way that I got round it, I called it the "Peter Pan principle" at the time,' said Tom's coach. 'He had to first of all recognize what the problem was, we'd send him away and he'd have a shower or a swim and he'd hopefully come back more controlled. The aim was to think happy thoughts. So that he could fly, as the Darling kids did within the Peter Pan story.' With the Peter Pan principle, Tom built confidence. However, his early fears are not uncommon. 'Most divers are really scared when they start diving,' he said. 'Because it's something that's not really natural. You don't really want to throw yourself off these diving boards that are so high. It's something that you kind of have to learn to deal with.'

He learned quickly enough to be thrown into competition before long. In September 2002, when it was deemed that Tom was ready to take part in real competition, he was placed into a suitable squad. By April of the following year, he was proudly clutching his first medal. The National Novice Championships of 2003 were the setting for his success. Competing in the 8–9 boys category, Tom did well enough to take a silver medal. This was, naturally, a confidence booster for him and also a proud moment for his family. Could Rob have guessed that in years to come he would be able to fill a room of their Plymouth home with medals that Tom would collect like a magnet?

Indeed, in September of the same year there were more medals to add to the by-now clinking collection. At an invitational event in Southampton, young Tom was in fine fettle. This time he literally struck gold, winning the top prize in the one-metre, three-metre and platform categories. Given the extent of his success in Southampton, it was already becoming clear that Tom was a special and determined boy. The days of him trembling with nerves at the Plymouth pool were already becoming a distant memory. Tom was collecting medals and enjoying himself as he did. Gradually, he and those around him felt their confidence levels rise.

By the end of 2003, Tom was a changed boy. Although at the start of the year he had still been making his first tentative steps into competitive diving, by the year's end he was already a medal-winning competitor. As he travelled round the country to diving events, he became very homesick, as any boy so young might, 'He'd phone us up crying, missing home,' remembered Rob. 'From then on we decided to go with him.'

It was a wise decision. One evening, after a gruelling day at a training camp, Andy Banks, Tom's coach since he was eight years old, recalled that Tom had been so upset that he made a dramatic threat. 'During the day he was fine,' said Banks in the *Daily Star*. 'During the evening the wheels fell off. Two of his statements to me were, "I would rather be dead than be on this training camp" and, "If you leave me alone in this room I will jump out of the window."' Banks said Tom's emotions were 'intense' and added that this outburst was 'pretty strong from a little kid in floods of tears, who was hanging on to the windowsill'. Tom's tormented state reminded everyone that, despite his maturity, he was still a young boy.

However, although he may have felt the pressure very intensely at times, the truth was that Tom was advancing rapidly. By any criteria – experience, confidence, medal-collection – he was doing well, and quickly. From the very start, Tom naturally held that vital quality in any champion: the stubborn refusal to ever be fully satisfied by any progress or success. With an appetite as ravenous as any natural champion's should be, he remained hungry for more and higher success.

In the summer of 2004, Tom became the under-18s platform diving champion of Britain. He was just ten years old and was getting noticed. 'The talent that Tom's got is simply unbelievable,' said the British Olympic swimmer Steve Parry, commenting on that remarkable achievement. Tom was the youngest ever winner of that event, making history even in his very early days. For some young athletes this could have become the defining moment of their career. It is all too easy at such a young age to become thrown off track by success, for the praise and wonder that they are inducing in others to go to their head. The sporting graveyard is full of 'big prospects' that never fulfilled people's expectations of them.

Tom and those around him had no intention of allowing this to happen to him, and seemed to be forever working harder and harder to improve. He was given a large trampoline for his tenth birthday, which was erected in the back garden and used to hone his technique.

He returned to Southampton for the 2004 invitational and – once again – was again on winning form. He won the under-11 one-metre springboard with 196.40 points, his nearest runner-up was local boy Chris Mears with 169.15 points. In the under-11 three-metre springboard he finished on top by a comfortable margin. With 205.50 points he was far ahead of the nearest runner-up, who was again Mears. In the boys 12–13 years platform he came equal first with Max Brick, another Southampton boy. It seemed that, whether competing against boys his own age or older, Tom was not just holding his own, but continually coming out on top.

And this would prove not just to be a flash in

the pan, instead Tom kept on competing against his elders. Other divers soon began to sigh with despair when they saw that Tom was included among their opponents. This fresh-faced boy from Plymouth might have looked as if butter would not melt in his mouth, but the truth was that when it came to the kill, he was as lethal as they came: rivals were tamed by his angelic face and tender years at their peril.

The 2005 ASA National Championships witnessed yet greater success for Tom. In the National Age Group competitions he was preeminent in three separate categories. In the 9–11 years contests he won on the one-metre, three-metre and platform categories with 246.30, 266.80 and 210.80 points respectively. When it came to the National Championships, he won the junior three-metre with 503.13 and came third in the junior platform with 500.79.

He also competed overseas, including in the German city of Aachen. On the western side of Germany, Aachen is a spa town that holds popular tennis and equestrian events. Tom arrived for the town's Junior International to compete against boys several years older than him, in the 14–15 years range. Even the Union flag that he carried into the pool area dwarfed little Tom. He did well, coming second in the platform with 350.85 points and third in the three-metre dive with a 367.45 total. He was given a pink flower on the podium.

Tom remembers this time with fondness and pride. 'I was on a winning streak, so my coach sent me to compete at Aachen, specifically in order to experience losing, but I came second, diving against fourteen- and fifteen-year-olds,' he said. 'So he sent me to another competition, again diving against older boys, and I won there as well.' He also participated in the Australian Elite Junior Nationals, where he was a guest competitor and again was battling against boys several years older than him. Once more, he did not allow their superior years and experience to intimidate him one bit. In the boys 14–15 platform contest it was Tom who held his nerve and won. His 418.98 points ensured he finished at the top of the pile Down Under, and the 474.09 he amassed in the three-metre gave him a second-placed finish. It had been a successful trip to Australia and he would make an even more successful return there in years to come.

•

Back home there was one more win for Tom when he came top in the British Championships junior platform. He had excelled during 2005, a year in which he served notice on the domestic and world stage that he was a force to be reckoned with. He began the year as a ten-year-old who was little known even in diving circles. As the year ended he was an eleven-year-old with a reputation in junior diving circles. Ever more fearless and focused, his determination and brilliant technique made him a threat to all opponents.

The year also cemented in Tom's mind that he deserved success. Few children his age got the chance to excel at anything outside of school, but Tom was already competing and succeeding. He was flying around the world and coming home with medals in his pocket. As important as the physical prizes were the emotional dividends that such wins offered. They brought him confidence and poise. Far from fanning the flames of ambition that burned within his soul, his haul of medals increased his determination to win.

During 2005 another key event occurred. In July at the 117th IOC Session in Singapore, it was announced that London's bid to hold the 2012 Olympic Games had been successful. Nine cities had originally bid to host the games, but in the final reckoning – after the bids from Moscow, New York, Havana, Istanbul, Leipzig, Rio de Janeiro and Madrid were all eliminated – it was a two-way fight between London and Paris. London called out the big guns to push home its bid, including football star David Beckham; while France threw its own football royalty behind the Paris bid in the form of World Cup star Zinedine Zidane and Laurent Blanc. Most people predicted that the Paris bid would succeed – in part because this was its third bid in recent history – but it was London that got the final nod, setting up the first Olympic Games to be held in this country since 1948.

IOC president Jacques Rogge made the dramatic announcement on 6 July. Thousands of flag-waving fans had gathered in Trafalgar Square in anticipation of the success. Among them were Olympians Kelly Holmes and Steve Cram. When the news was broken, the crowd exploded with delight. There were cheers, tears of joy and dancing as tickertape and balloons filled the air. 'It is absolutely incredible,' said double gold-medallist Holmes. 'I know how passionate it is to be involved in the Olympics.' Cram was so excited that he joked, 'I'm thinking of coming out of retirement!' Swimmer Sharron Davies added, 'We will be showing off Britain like never before.' As news spread across the country, there was so much excitement, joy and anticipation.

Back at the scene of the official announcement, Olympic athlete and chair of the organising committee for London 2012, Sebastian Coe said, 'This is just the most fantastic opportunity to do everything we ever dreamed of in British sport.' Her Majesty The Queen sent Coe a message of praise and celebration. 'I send my warmest congratulations to you and every member of the London 2012 team for winning the bid for the

UK,' it read. 'It's a really outstanding achievement to beat such a highly competitive field.'

Then Prime Minister Tony Blair broke away from a meeting at the G8 summit at Gleneagles to call it a 'momentous day' for all of Britain. He added, 'Many reckon [London] is the greatest capital city in the world and the Olympics will help keep it that way.' The gloss was taken off the announcement when, the following day, a series of terrorist attacks hit the capital. But they could not change the fact that the Olympics were coming to London.

For Tom, the news of London's successful bid was music to his ears. He knew that by the time the tournament started he would have recently turned eighteen. The fact he would reach such a milestone in the same year that the Olympic Games came to Britain was, he thought, surely no coincidence. It felt as if fate was at his side, leading him to a summer of destiny in 2012. Although the tournament was at this stage some seven years away, for Tom it must have felt as if he could reach out and touch the excitement, opportunity and glory it would offer him. The knowledge that the tournament would be held in Britain further fuelled his dreams and ambition. Had Paris have been chosen to host the Olympics he would still have wanted to participate and win, but the chance to win gold for his country on his home soil was, obviously, special.

Times of high excitement for the diver from Devon, and the song that reminds Tom of this period of his life is 'Proud' by Heather Small. It is one of his favourite songs. 'It . . . makes me think of that amazing moment in July 2005 when it was announced that we'd beaten Paris and would be hosting the games. And it is also a song that I listen to when I am competing.' The perfect song for those who strive to ever better themselves, it's no wonder Tom loves it. 'What have you done today to make you feel proud?' asks the chorus over and over. Tom can almost always answer positively, but he does not use the song to pat himself on the back, rather he makes it push him further forward. 'It motivates me to work harder during training to try to reach that big ambition of winning an Olympic gold medal – perhaps in London 2012,' he said of Small's song.

If 2005 had been a pivotal year for young Tom, in 2006 he was to enjoy more success in his quest to become Britain's leading diver. It was becoming increasingly clear that there was nothing ordinary about this remarkable boy from Devon. His life was very different to that of other children of his age – his 'normal' home, family and school life contrasted sharply with his increasingly international profile, competing in events both all around Britain and overseas. For now, this would not present many problems for him but in just a few years, he would begin to see that standing out from the crowd was not always a positive or enjoyable experience. Indeed, reality would soon be setting in on Tom from several fronts. How he responded to the challenges of the years immediately ahead would decide how great a talent he could become, and just what a remarkable soul he is.

The stakes were high, and nobody was ignoring the reality of what Tom would have to do to fulfil the potential that had been identified in him. Then British Diving's national performance director, Steve Foley, explained what was expected of Tom, now that he was a full member of the Olympic junior diving programme. 'If you've got a twelve-year-old and your asking for a commitment of six more years, at the moment that's half their life,' said Foley. 'That's a big ask for anyone. At the end of the day whoever wants it that much more will have the edge.' Tom could scarcely want it more than he already did.

•

In 2006 Tom experienced contrasting fortunes. He continued to win medals and star at tournaments, but he also faced some challenges both in diving and in his personal life. For some time, things had seemed to go like a dream. This was the year that true reality would set in as he realized that life consisted – both metaphorically and literally – of ups and downs. He won in three categories at the ASA Elite Junior Nationals and finished first and second in two at the ASA National Championships. In the Junior tournament he had competed in the 12–13 years slot and won in the one-metre, three-metre and platform events. His highest point tally came in the platform, where he amassed 362.90 points. In the National Championships he was in the junior slot and won the three-metre event with 285.45, finishing runner-up with 388.55 in the platform. His next trip to Germany for the Aachen Junior International proved less successful than the previous year. Up against boys as old as fifteen, he could only finish eighth in the three-metre dive, but again the trip had been a valuable experience. True champions learn from disappointments every bit as keenly as they celebrate triumphs.

He also faced a fresh and considerable crisis of confidence during the year. During the spring months he was learning two new dives – a back three-and-a-half somersaults and inward three-and-a-half somersaults. Suddenly, he lost his nerve. To his surprise, he felt entirely unable to climb the ladders up to the diving platform. He withdrew from one competition at the last moment after panicking about his new dives. He thought this marked the end for him. 'I thought I would never be able to go back up there on a ten-metre board again, I thought I'd be too scared,' he explained. 'Not just for those dives but for anything.'

For a while, he admitted, this did not feel like it was going to be a passing obstacle, but a permanent barrier. 'I just couldn't do them and I didn't know why. Perhaps if I'd had a psychologist there to talk to or somebody there I could trust, like my coach, but I felt I was on my own. I just couldn't face going up there.' It took months for him to return to his usual level of confidence.

This had not been the first time that Tom had crumbled in the face of a challenge. 'When he first came to do a back spin off the three metres (board) he was hiding behind the pillar, taking big breaths, crying a little, walking back and forth,' explained Andy Banks. 'Finally he did it and now he is so comfortable with how a back spin works that he will do it off the ten-metre board without a worry. There was a time when he didn't want to learn anything new. It was only when he learned a reverse dive and realized he could do it that the learning curve went vertical.'

As before, Tom dug deep and eventually found the strength to conquer his fears. He gave it another go – and another and another – until finally he could do it with complete confidence. Learning a new dive is no small feat, sometimes it can take an athlete several months to perfect a new move. The rewards for their determination can be huge.

Tom was in better form at the British Championships where he finished first in the junior platform and junior three-metre. More impressive still was his third-placed ranking in the senior platform. It was proving a good year for Tom as his confidence and achievements grew. There was a price for his success and he often missed out on things that boys his age would normally have been enjoying. 'I miss out on things all the time because of training – sometimes I get invited to barbecues or parties and I can't go – but you have to make sacrifices,' he said. 'My dream is to win gold in London 2012.'

Tom was lucky in that as his success grew, he attracted the attention of people who could help guide and mentor him. These included one of his idols, Leon Taylor, who had won a silver medal in synchronized diving at the Athens Olympics in 2004. 'He has the magic ingredient which you can't define. I don't want to call it an X-factor but that's what it is,' Taylor said in an interview for the BBC. 'Tom is capable of really great things – what is happening is very, very special – but it's important everyone doesn't get too excited too soon.'

Taylor expanded more specifically on what he was hoping to be able to offer Tom. 'The reason I wanted to be involved is that I want to give Tom the best chance possible to be as successful as he can be,' he said. 'I can share experiences with him which other people can't. For example, at school there is going to be jealousy and envy of his achievements within the sport. You have to be humble about it, which isn't a problem for Tom because he is not cocky or big-headed.'

Tom was indeed an unassuming soul in many ways but even eschewing the temptation to be cocky or big-headed would not be enough to protect him when, as Taylor had predicted, life at school became a challenge as the green-eyed monster reared its ugly head. Meanwhile, expanding on how the coming years might look for Tom, Taylor spoke of more challenges that lay ahead for him. 'There's a long road ahead of Tom, he's got growth spurts to deal with and girls are going to come into the equation, these are all distractions.' Hinting at where his input could be invaluable, should Tom seek it, Taylor added, 'So it's a case of Tom making the right choices at the right time.'

Meanwhile, Tom had a fresh and painful challenge to face. In 2006, his parents received some terrible news. Rob had been feeling out of sorts for some time, and when he surrendered himself to a medical check-up, the news was not good – he had cancer. Remembering the circumstances of the diagnosis, Rob spoke with characteristic light wit. 'I was getting confused, depressed, which isn't like me,' he told the BBC. 'They did tests, then told me I was walking around with a brain tumour the size of a grapefruit in my head. No one wants to hear that.'

No one indeed, least of all the children of the sufferer – and the next challenge for Rob and his wife was for them to decide when and how to break the news to the children. This was not an easy thing to keep quiet. Quite apart from the dreadful news itself, there was the fact that Rob would have to have his head shaved for the operation to remove the tumour. However, the couple struck upon a ruse that would mean they could keep the horrible truth from their children for a while at least.

'It was around the time of Comic Relief, so I said I'd shaved my head for charity,' Rob remembered in the *Daily Mail*. 'Next day, I went into hospital for the op, but we told them it was for tests. When I came out, we said they'd had to do a little procedure, so the boys couldn't jump on me for a bit.' These 'white lies' allowed the Daleys to keep the news to themselves while they absorbed the shock, and while they waited for further news on Rob's condition. When they were ready to share the news, they told the kids. Asked how Tom reacted, Rob said, 'Like everything, really. He took it in his stride.'

Such news will have given Tom much cause for reflection, though, as watching anyone close to you – let alone a parent – battling cancer brings a huge dose of perspective into one's own life – a quality teenagers are usually short of. All of Tom's behaviour since the news of his father's illness was broken to him should be considered through this prism. Sensing how tenuous a human's grasp on life can be, he has approached life with added zeal and determination.

Naturally, this new determination and vigour allowed him to build on his already considerable successes in diving and take his progress to a whole new level. Already, Tom had made the diving world sit up and take notice. Quickly, he would also capture the attention and hearts of the nation at large. More than that, his fame was now beginning to become global.

However, as he reflected over the events of 2006 and looked ahead to the year to come, Tom could surely not have predicted the shockwaves he was going to send through the sport.

CHAPTER FOUR

•

International Bright Young Thing

'The AYOF [Australian Youth Olympic Festival] motto
is "see tomorrow's Olympians today", and Thomas is
certainly heading that way.'
**CRAIG PHILLIPS, secretary general of the Australian
Olympic Committee**

TOM'S RISE IN THE DIVING WORLD coincided with a
positive development in the sport, as increased funding
from the National Lottery began to transform it. Some
£4.6 million was pumped into diving from lottery
funds, via the Performance Pathway route. Some of
this found its way to the English Institute of Sport
facilities in Plymouth, thus directly benefiting Tom.
Also of local and direct benefit to Tom was the £34,000
lottery funding received by Central Park Pool.

'Without the lottery funding our athletes would
never have been able to catch up with the rest of the
world,' said Leon Taylor. He went on to explain how

young talent such as Tom would be a force for good. 'Beijing is going to be tough. To topple the Chinese in China will be a grand task. People have retired, there's a cloud hanging over me and it is up to the younger ones to carry the mantle. But after that it looks really positive with Tom and the young whippersnappers coming through. I haven't the words to describe what it will be like as a British athlete when the Olympics come to London. I wish I was Tom's age working towards it.'

Throughout 2007, Tom continued to work towards just that. The year began with a sensational development. In January, Tom received the exciting news that he was being given a special dispensation to take part in the Australian Youth Olympic Festival. At twelve years of age he was outside the age range for the tournament, which is usually restricted to people between the ages of fourteen and nineteen, but when the British Olympic Association had requested of its Australian counterparts in June 2006 that Tom be allowed to join the festival, he was given the green light.

'Given his results we could hardly refuse the request,' said AOC secretary general, Craig Phillips. 'The AYOF motto is "see tomorrow's Olympians today", and Thomas is certainly heading that way.' He joined 105 other Team GB athletes to compete in the tournament in Sydney. How excited he was as his plane took off for the lengthy flight to Australia. Among his British teammates for the trip was fellow diver Tonia Couch, with whom he has a sibling-like relationship, Tom the younger brother to Tonia the elder sister.

The only thing that marred his excitement was that he was still being troubled by a persistent thumb injury, a clear handicap to a diver (if you are not sure of that, then try hitting water at a speed of thirty miles an hour with a hand injury – you'll quickly understand). When he first learned what his injury could mean for his progress, Tom cried. However, not for the final time in his career, he overcame this disadvantage and did himself justice. He would acquire the nickname 'Tom Thumb' in time, but this setback was no laughing matter.

His elevation, though, was interestingly timed. Following the England team's poor performance at the 2006 World Cup Finals, there had been hopes that our rugby side or cricketers could restore national pride at their own events. The England rugby team was similarly humiliated in the autumn rugby series. Then came the Ashes, in which the Australian cricket team not only defeated England, but did so via a 5-0 whitewash. The English public wondered if we would ever excel in sports again. In this atmosphere, the public were willing to look to any sport for hope. So as Tom travelled to Australia – the scene of England's most recent sporting disaster – for the Australian Youth Olympic Festival, there was more interest than there would normally be for a twelve-year-old diver. Also alongside him was another fellow Plymouth sporting star, sixteen-year-old skeet shooter marksman, Rory Warlow.

The fact Tom had been given special dispensation to take part in the tournament guaranteed a whirlwind of media interest around him from the moment he set foot in Australia. All the excitement could not hide the challenges that lay ahead for him as he acclimatized to a warmer country and recovered from the combined vigour of a long flight and a radically different time zone.

This was just the start of it. For Tom, the most immediate challenge facing him was overcoming a stomach muscle strain. 'Tom has been struggling a bit with his stomach – it's a ligament problem he picked up in the national championships,' said Andy Banks. He added that this ligament problem was not expected to be anything that the youngster could not overcome in time to participate. 'He's been having physiotherapy and has been training hard, so I don't think it will prevent him from competing in the individual ten-metre competition or the synchro. Both Tonia and Tom are enjoying the facilities here in Sydney, which are absolutely superb. They should both go into tomorrow's synchronized competition with high hopes of doing well.'

Tom was very excited about the prospect of this

tournament. Having been allowed to take part in a contest for which he was too young to qualify, he faced two possible outcomes. Either he could justify the optimism and faith that had been instilled in him, or he could fall flat on his face and confirm the scepticism of anyone who had doubted the wisdom of his inclusion at such a tender age.

Tom took the high road, and won silver in Sydney. Brushing aside the multitude of factors against him – his tender years, the injury worry during the tournament build-up among them – and finishing second.

Back home in Devon, the locals were immensely proud of their increasingly famous son. However, even here, the local politics of the sport were never far beneath the celebratory surface. 'Great praise to the pair of them and also to coaches Andy Banks and Sam Grevett, who have produced Tom, Tonia and lots more excellent divers, despite having to train at the Mayflower Centre, which is well past its sell-by date,' cheered the *Plymouth Herald*. For Tom, that issue could wait its turn. He had flown across the world, taken part in a tournament for which he was far too young, and finished with a silver medal. Life felt very good indeed, and this was just the start of Tom's cross-continental journey.

For then it was on to Canada, where Tom was scheduled to take part in another prestigious tournament. At the Canada Cup Grand Prix in Montreal he made his senior international debut. The Canada event is one of the best-attended swimming grand prix of the year, and there he rubbed shoulders with junior world medallists and senior world championships finalists. Wherever he turned his bright brown eyes there were top-class, medal-winning competitors for them to feast upon. So he could be more than excused for an attack of nerves, especially as he had to dive first in the semi-finals.

The order in which divers dive can be crucial, and for young Tom, making his senior international debut, diving first at the semi-final stage meant he had no target to aim at. He was truly coming of age and conquering his nerves as he went along – the mark of a true champion. He admitted that it was not just during the semi-finals that he felt anxious. 'Yes, that was a bit scary, but then I was quite nervous in the preliminaries too,' Tom told the *Plymouth Herald*. 'But once the competition got underway and I had dived, I felt all right and really enjoyed taking part. I hadn't really worried too much about the Olympic qualifying mark, but I must admit it's really nice to have got it at my first attempt.'

Naturally, he relished the experience in Canada. As much as anything, Tom was excited that he had had the opportunity to speak to one of his long-term heroes, though reminders of his own tender years were never far away. 'It was also really nice to speak to Alexandre [Despatie], who is my idol and who has been very nice to me and given me time and advice. It was quite funny at times because lots of people kept coming up and asking me "how old are you?"'

It is good that Tom was able to find this amusing. His precocious talent meant he would often rub shoulders with older and more experienced athletes, so observations about the gulf in their ages would be something that would be made for a while. Once they finished, Tom would know he had not only 'arrived' in terms of years, but also that his remarkably swift rise had become something people were less surprised by. Instead, they began to expect that he would excel – and that would mean he had *truly* arrived.

Suddenly, an even more amazing prospect appeared to be on the cards for Tom: a place in the 2008 summer Olympics Games. To be held in Beijing, China, these games were going to attract over 11,000 athletes from around the world, with over 302 separate events scheduled across the sixteen-day tournament. Could it be that Tom would be one of the 11,000 taking part in the diving leg of those events? During 2007, he increasingly realized that this could be the case and that the Olympics could be a possibility for him. 'Yes, I think they probably are,' he said. Remembering to keep his feet on the ground and his eyes focused, he added: 'But I'm looking forward to the rest of the year and the other senior events and being more experienced for the British trials in January [2008].'

Plymouth Diving coach Sam Grevett agreed that a place at the China games was a realistic prospect for Tom, who was just days away from his thirteenth birthday as Grevett made this statement. The remarkable nature of his progress continued to astound. 'Tom is still only twelve and too young even to compete in major junior international competitions,' she said. 'But British Diving have agreed to give him the opportunity to learn his trade on the senior circuit, where there is no minimum age restriction. Next year will be the first year that Tom is eligible to compete at major championships. While a medal at 2012 had always been his goal, a place on the 2008 team is not unrealistic.'

More immediately, he eyed his forthcoming challenge in Madrid at the Spanish Grand Prix in June. Tonia Couch, meanwhile, had her eyes set on Germany where the Grand Prix would take place at Rostock later in June.

Before any of that, there was a significant boost to Tom's prospects when, the week following his thirteenth birthday, it was announced that he had been personally selected by Olympic legends Sir Steve Redgrave and Dame Tanni Grey-Thompson to join up with sixteen of the country's most talented athletes for a key sponsorship deal. He was included in the exclusive *Team Visa* programme unveiled at Lord's cricket ground in May. This important programme was created to assist the athletes considered most likely to take part in the Beijing 2008 and London 2012 Olympic and Paralympic Games.

The benefits for Tom were so much more than monetary. Under this scheme he and the other fifteen athletes selected had Redgrave and Grey-Thompson installed as official mentors. They were to be always available at the end of the phone for any advice or guidance Tom needed, or even just for a generally encouraging chat. These were expert mentors to have: Redgrave won gold medals at five consecutive Olympic Games and has also won three Commonwealth medals. Grey-Thompson, meanwhile, is arguably Britain's finest ever Paralympics athlete, who has been awarded both an MBE and an OBE for her contribution to British sport.

In return for this, and for the sponsorship from Visa, Tom agreed to make five public appearances, which included opening shopping centres and autograph sessions. For Tom, these were not problematic demands. He was becoming increasingly fond of the attention that fame brought him. Indeed, he was even looking ahead to how he could use this fame beyond his diving career. His key ambition was to become a television presenter. So being in front of the cameras at Lord's for the launch of the Visa sponsorship was great for him. 'It was a big occasion with all the national TV and press there, so it was great being involved along with the other young athletes,' he said. 'I hadn't been to Lord's before and had never met Sir Steve or Dame Tanni, although I've seen them competing lots of times on TV . . . It was fantastic to have both Sir Steve and Dame Tanni as my personal mentors – they are both legends. I spoke to them for quite a while and they told me about their experiences as international athletes and how they coped at the Olympics and Paralympics. We got on really well with them and I even made Sir Steve laugh when I said that one of my ambitions was to beat his gold medal record. Just being able to talk to them from time to time is really good, too.' He added: 'Their support and encouragement can only help my development as an athlete and [Olympic] prospect.'

As for Redgrave, he was not at all put out by Daley's stated ambition. 'Thomas is a terrifically talented performer and it will be very rewarding for me personally to have played a part in his progress,' he said.

One of the times that Tom took advantage of his relationship with Redgrave was when he found he was having trouble sleeping ahead of important competitions. He picked up the phone and asked

Redgrave if he had ever suffered from pre-tournament insomnia. 'He said he did, but that you don't need that much sleep to perform at your best, so that was a help,' said Tom.

Rob was delighted for Tom. His first emotion was one of paternal pride, but underneath this was also a keen and canny grasp on what this would mean in practical terms. 'This is very, very good news for Tom as it is his first major sponsorship,' Rob said. 'We've had help over the past eighteen months from my brother-in-law, Kevin, whose firm Airtech have given us a Volkswagen Transporter to travel around in. Hopefully, Visa will be the first of many sponsorship deals and are sure to raise Tom's profile.'

This was a key issue for Tom, as it is for any diver. In contrast to sports such as motor racing and football, where leading competitors can make literally millions of pounds in such deals every year, diving is not a sport in which sponsorship opportunities excel. Tom's other sponsors are the kit manufacturer Adidas, he is a member of Team Nestlé, and also has deals with British Swimming and the lottery-funded UK Sport.

Both Rob and Tom were anxious to grab appropriate financial opportunities when they arose – and with good reason. It was all very well being successful and famous for now, but Tom also had to think long-term and pragmatically too. Even in the meantime, there were issues to be addressed. The Daley family were only able to travel to China to watch Tom in the 2008 Olympics thanks to two companies stepping in to cover their air fares. As for tickets to the events themselves, Rob had to pay for them like any other spectator. For the World Cup meetings, also in Beijing, it had been even worse: Rob had been forced to buy tickets from a tout, just to watch his own son dive.

When Tom was asked how he felt about this surprising state of affairs, he played a straight bat. 'I don't think he minds,' he told *The Independent*. 'He comes everywhere to watch me dive.' Behind this statement there must have been some frustration in the Daley family that they had to pay for their own tickets. In most sports, including football, players are given at least a couple of complimentary tickets for each match. Often much more.

•

But before he could start focusing on Beijing, there was the Spanish Grand Prix in Madrid to contend with, where Tom came agonizingly close to a medal. Ticking off yet another fascinating, exciting city on his list of places that his diving had taken him, he was enthralled by the Spanish capital. However, while he took a great deal of pleasure and experience from the trip, he was not able to finish on the podium, coming fourth in the final of the men's platform event. Given that he was up against an experienced set of opponents, this was a major achievement for young Tom. It was a close finish, in which he was separated from a bronze medal by just six points. To complete the impressive picture, this was still only his second senior international tournament.

Tom reacted to his achievement with the mixture of pride and disappointment that any competitive, ambitious athlete would feel. 'I'm obviously delighted with my diving and coming fourth, but I still believe I could have come back with a bronze medal,' he said. 'In fact, I'm very disappointed really, but overall I'm just as happy at how things went for me. I had been in the silver medal position going into the fourth dive in the final but, unfortunately, I missed that one, as I was starting to get tired. But I'll learn from that, I'm learning all the time, I pick up something new at every big competition I go to.'

Tom's reaction is revealing. He was aware that he had achieved something very special for a boy of his age and experience, yet he felt disappointment that he had not done better. He is not one to settle for what he perceives as 'second best'. However, he is also not one to flounce off in a prolonged huff. Instead, he played back in his mind what had happened during the tournament and asked himself what lessons he could learn for the future. All of these characteristics are the marks of a true champion. His ability as a diver is obviously the central gift he has. Arguably just as important though is what goes on in his mind and how he greets both good and bad developments along the way. Psychology is an increasingly recognized factor in all sports. Given that diving is for the most part an individual sport, and one that requires a high level of confidence, the mentality of the participant becomes all the more important.

The mathematics show just how close he had come. He had won the semi-final with a mighty score of 450. In the final – his first in a senior tournament – he competed against five other divers. The winner was Liguang Yang of China, with his fellow countryman Hu Jia second. Tom got 419.7 points, which left him just short of his Ukrainian rival Kostyantyn Milyaev's score of 425.7.

While many of Tom's coaching team had been at pains to encourage him to keep his feet on the ground, they had to admit that he was surpassing expectations. 'He's surprising everyone, not just at our club but also on the international circuit, every time he competes,' said Plymouth Diving coach Sam Grevett. 'Tom's goal had always been 2012, but with performances like this, Beijing is certainly beckoning.'

The excitement was tangible and understandable,

what was vital was that it did not have a negative effect on Tom himself. Showing that he had an older head on his young shoulders, he tried to bring some caution to the party. 'Going to Beijing is starting to look a reality for me, but I'm not getting carried away,' said Daley. 'I look at it this way: if I make the Olympics next year, great, if I don't then it's not the end of the world. I know I will have done my best to try and qualify, as I do at every tournament I compete in. In Madrid, in the preliminaries, I dived better than I had done before at that standard of competition. That has given me a lot of confidence.' So it should have done. It became increasingly clear that Tom, who had for so long built his dream around making his Olympic debut at the 2012 Olympic Games, was now on course to take his bow in that tournament four years earlier than planned.

Meantime, his soaring fortunes were attracting increasing attention and recognition. In December 2007 Tom became the youngest ever winner of the *Plymouth Herald* Sports Personality of the Year award. 'Just being nominated, let alone winning, is a fantastic feeling,' said Tom looking back. 'The *Herald* awards evenings are really special. It gives local sportsmen and women the chance to meet up and get to know each other.' He also became the subject of a semi-regular feature on BBC television, becoming one of the athletes BBC Sport followed as part of the *Olympics Dreams* series. Here, following the progress of a variety of Olympic hopefuls, viewers were given a glimpse into Tom's everyday life, thanks to on-the-spot reports from presenter Gaby Logan, who spoke with Tom and his parents. 'He's enjoyed success from an early age,' said Rob. 'He's enjoyed getting medals and winning competitions. So that's driven him.'

Tom's mother was asked about what food fuelled the family's young athlete. 'Obviously I'd rather he ate something healthy rather than crisps and biscuits,' said Debbie. 'So I give him some scrambled eggs and toast – a healthy option.' However, she admitted that she did not always manage to keep to such nutritional standards. Rob added that he did the shopping and also tried his best to bring healthy, appropriate food into the home. He said that the kids got through so much food it was 'like having three men in the house – or four men should I say, including myself!'

Logan was then shown upstairs by Tom. Noting the walls were painted red, she told him that the colour red is considered very lucky in China. 'Is it?' he said, excitedly. 'Well, hopefully . . . maybe, maybe,' he added.

Tom then proudly showed her his growing collection of medals, choosing the British Men's Platform title medal as his favourite. Explaining the attraction of diving for him he spoke of the 'adrenaline rush' it afforded him, and said 'It's like being on a rollercoaster, like being at a fairground'. Comparing the dive to doing a 'loop the loop on the rollercoaster', he said that it retained that sense of excitement and edge however many times he repeated it.

Tom's next honour was another from the BBC – and was a real honour in every sense of the word: the 2007 BBC Young Sports Personality of the Year. Past winners of this prestigious award included football star Wayne Rooney, tennis player Andy Murray, and swimmer Kate Haywood. The previous year's winner was Arsenal and England starlet Theo Walcott. Prior to Tom's winning, never before had a diver landed the gong. He was not at the ceremony, as the host, Sue Barker, explained: 'Such is the dedication and workload of our top three contenders that I'm afraid none of them can be here tonight,' said Barker. However, Tom had recorded a message of acceptance and it was shown to the admiring audience.

'I'm sorry I can't be with you guys in Birmingham,' said Tom. 'I'd just like to thank the judging panel for giving me this award, and I'd like to thank my coach for believing in me and getting me through the ups and downs of my diving career so far.' He also thanked his mother and father 'for ferrying me around', and his school. He added that his next goal was to go to the 2008 Olympics, then to win a medal at London 2012 –

'and make my parents proud'.

As the Sports Personality of the Year show was aired, Tom was busy doing what he does best – diving. He was in Montreal, Canada, competing at the CAMO Invitational Meeting, the eleventh time that tournament had been held. He dived in the 10-metre synchro, alongside Blake Aldridge. Interestingly, their main rivals on the day were another British partnership – Leon Taylor and Peter Waterfield, winners of the pairs synchro silver medal at the Athens Olympics in 2004. When it came to the crunch in Canada, Tom and Blake were very impressive. Their performance included a perfect 10, and in the end they beat the Taylor–Waterfield partnership by less than eight points. It was a tight margin, but margin enough for Tom and his partner to take gold.

It was the first time that a British pair had beaten Taylor–Waterfield for ten years. Incredible stuff – and all this on the same day that he was being named the BBC's Young Sports Personality of the Year back in London. With Christmas just eight days away, the festive season was indeed turning into one of cheer for Tom. The future seemed just as cheerful. 'My next focus will be to qualify for the World Cup in Beijing so I have the chance to qualify for the Olympics,' said Tom, looking ahead to 2008. 'It would be amazing to go to an Olympics at fourteen.'

It really would . . .

CHAPTER FIVE

•

Beijing and Beyond

'Just enjoy every minute of it and try to remember as
much of it as you can.'
KENNETH LESTER, the youngest ever Olympian

In 2008, Tom and his fellow Plymouth diver Sarah
Barrow were part of an eleven-strong Great Britain
squad who competed against other World Cup Beijing
hopefuls in the first leg of the three-day FINA Grand
Prix series. Due to join them was Plymouth's Brooke
Graddon, however unfortunately she had to drop out of
the squad due to a cold bug. She had only just bounced
back from prolonged injury and illness problems,
so she was devastated to not be joining her friends.
While Barrow dived alongside Monique McCarroll
of Southampton, Tom competed in the synchro event,
along with Blake Aldridge, and also in the individual
competition. 'It's going to be another tough competition
because there are divers just as keen as us to do well,'

said Daley ahead of the action. 'Although there isn't going to be the pressure on us, as there will be in the World Cup, it's still a grand prix meet and will be a very good standard. There will be pressure from ourselves to do well. Hopefully, Blake and myself will do well in the synchro and I can get into the individual finals.'

Coach Andy Banks put the event in context: 'The Madrid meet is a really good way of the team ticking over against some high-class divers, all with the same thought in mind. With the World Cup coming up next month, they will be making sure their standards don't drop.'

On Saturday's synchro event Tom and Blake did well enough to grab a silver medal. Barrow and McCarroll had grabbed a silver as well, making it a great haul for the Plymouth contingent.

However, it was in the individual round that Tom tasted most drama. The gold and silver places were claimed early by Chinese divers Hu Jia and Liguang Yang. This left an all-British face-off for bronze between Tom and Southampton's experienced Peter Waterfield. Having scored four 10s in the first round, Tom was in a good position. Waterfield felt the pressure and fluffed his back two-and-a-half somersaults and two-and-a-half twists piked.

Tom scented blood and took full advantage, pulling off his back three-and-a-half tuck in style. 'I'm over the moon,' he said. 'The way that Pete is diving, I never expected to beat him today.' He finished with a total of 495.45 points, which was his personal best by 10 points. 'One of Tom's goals was to try and up his game from the prelims to the semis and then the final,' Andy Banks told the *Plymouth Herald*. 'Historically, he also did great in the prelims and then tired, but this time he managed to improve each time. He set a personal best in the semi and then beat that in the final, which was great. The synchro event also went really well for him and Blake. That was really important with the World Cup coming up where Britain need a top eight finish to get an Olympic place. It was a good weekend all round for Britain, but particularly for Plymouth with us having two divers competing and winning three medals.'

He also took part in the European Championships in Eindhoven. 'Afterwards, we had a really cool party in a nightclub, which I was allowed to go to even though I'm only thirteen,' he wrote in his diary for the *Daily Mail*. However, as he went on to explain, he was soon sent crashing back down to earth by the realities of family life. 'The next day, it was into the car and home with my family. My two little brothers had come to watch and they said well done, but they tell everyone else I'm rubbish at diving!' All good family fun, but luckily the selectors saw Tom's incredible talent and he was officially selected and qualified to represent Britain at the 2008 Olympic Games in Beijing. His place was confirmed during the Diving World Cup, also held in Beijing. 'He hugged me so tight and I hugged him back,' recalled Rob. 'I was flooding with tears.'

No wonder father and son were so excited. At just fourteen years of age, Tom would be competing at the highest event of his sport. Once more, he was punching above his weight. The world would be watching and overnight he would go from a boy well known in the world's diving community, to a boy known by the globe's general public.

But anyone who thought Tom might be overawed by the Olympics experience was mistaken. He took easily to the pressures and attention that came with participation in the tournament. More than ever before, he showed how at ease he was in a high profile, adult environment. Rarely had such a young athlete been so at home under the spotlight. 'I'm absolutely thrilled that I am going to an Olympics,' he said. 'I thought I would get to the London Olympics but not Beijing. I just can't wait until August.'

However, his easy-going and mature nature did not mean the trip was without controversy. For the first time in his career, Tom was to become embroiled in some uncomfortable headlines.

First, though, came the process of getting his head

around what lay ahead for him. Despite his confidence and maturity, it still took a bit of processing for him. 'I didn't expect at all to be taking part in this Olympics,' he said. 'I was more expecting London 2012. So when I qualified it was a big shock to me even though I had worked hard for an outside chance. I didn't expect to be pre-selected at the first instance.' Added Tom: 'It's going to be a massive challenge but it's going to be so much fun and I've got nothing to lose out there. I'm really looking forward to getting out there, doing the whole Olympic experience, staying in the Olympic village and competing in the Olympic venues, so it should be really good fun.'

Still, even though he had masses of exciting new experiences to come, he could calm himself by remembering that certain things were the same. 'The only thing that all diving boards have in common is that they are ten metres high,' he said. 'They've got different surfaces on them, different surroundings. When you're spinning around you need to be able to see the ceiling so if that's higher that changes things. For instance in Beijing they've got a fifteen-metre board above a ten-metre board. You need to be able to spot, and to come out at the right places.' He added: 'I'm as ready as I'll ever be, I guess. I've been training hard for it . . . so I'm basically now in hard training until the Olympics.' He was looking forward to the experience, and all it would bring with it, particularly relishing the prospect of speaking with athletes from other countries. 'If I came back with a medal it would be the best thing that had ever happened to me. To be able to say I'd won an Olympic medal, that's not something that happens to everyone so that would be really good.'

So off he flew to Beijing, another long-haul flight for Britain's exciting teenage prospect. Tom's fairy tale story had captured many a heart. Brits felt enamoured and excited by Tom so he carried with him the hopes of many British people. Some also felt protective towards him, unable to bear the idea that he might not succeed. Fortunately, he was not short of people looking out for him. The British officials were a well of encouragement and advice. 'I told him, "Embrace the Olympics, don't let the Olympics embrace you",' said Steve Foley, the national performance director for diving. 'That means go and experience it. Go and find out for yourself.'

Tom's family also travelled to Beijing, and indulged in some sightseeing at the Forbidden City and the Great Wall of China to break up what was a lengthy stay. 'It has been a long time,' said Rob. On Tom's insistence, the family also visited the Olympic village. 'When we got there I was gobsmacked,' said Rob. 'I have never seen anything like it. It was awesome.'

At the games themselves, Tom was in his element. Beijing's opening ceremony was one of the high points of his life. His every move seemed to be being documented by the media. He was regularly interviewed, and in one such chat with the BBC early on in his stay he was asked what he had been doing so far in Beijing. 'Training,' he said wistfully. 'That's pretty much it – training.' He was reminded that he had enjoyed a day out. 'Oh yeah, we went out to the Great Wall . . . so that's good,' he suddenly remembered. 'We went up in a cable car and came down on a toboggan. Brilliant.'

He was also featured cutting rings out of pieces of paper of different colours, to construct his own 'Olympic rings' logo. He explained that the waiting time was an essentially positive thing for him. 'There's been a big gap but that's good because it means I've been able to wind down and then build into a competition like I normally would, so it's been good.' To help him wind down, Tom spent a lot of time playing on games consoles and watching television.

The BBC camera crew that followed him around the Olympic village increasingly built a sense of how very much at ease Tom was with media attention. Footage showed him getting off the coach, dark glasses on, looking every inch the modern celebrity. He was caught on camera failing spectacularly at a bowling alley and on a golf driving range. It was all good-humoured stuff. So much did he love the camera's attention that, as one of his teammates was being interviewed, Tom could be seen in the background of the shot, jumping up and down on a trampoline, waving and smiling at the camera, even at one point sticking out his tongue. There was – quite literally on this occasion – no keeping this boy down.

Asked what the best part of the Olympic village was, Tom replied, 'I'd say the games room is pretty cool.' Talk often turned to the games room during the BBC filming. At one point he promised to take on a cameraman there, adding, 'Of course I'll beat you,' ever the competitive soul. The word 'brilliant' became his signature response to most questions. So full of positivity and enthusiasm was Tom, that when asked how anything was going, or how much he was enjoying anything, he more often than not responded 'brilliant!'. A reporter cheekily asked Tom whether it was 'a bit sad' that when he played on the X-Box in the games room, he was usually playing a 'diving' game. Tom was having none of this, replying that it was no more strange than a real-life footballer playing a football computer game.

The overall impression was of a teenage boy loving every minute of the experience. 'He's a kid in a chocolate factory,' said Steve Foley. 'He's having a ball, and he's not overawed at all.'

Soon, the competition would start for him, and with that in mind, Tom had been given advice by Kenneth

Lester, who had himself become an Olympian at the age of thirteen. 'Just enjoy every minute of it and try to remember as much of it as you can,' advised Lester, who had been the cox during the Rome Olympics in 1960. Lester later spoke with a combination of modesty and admiration of Tom's precocious maturity. Asked what other advice he had offered Tom, Lester said, 'I don't know about me advising him – he was minding me!'

One of the differences between the experience of the Olympics enjoyed by Lester, and that which was around the corner for Tom, was that Lester had always regretted that his own Olympic journey was not better documented in text or photograph. For a camera-happy athlete in the twenty-first century such as Tom, this would never be an issue.

Indeed, the growing media interest in Tom, and the challenges that it brought with it, were being noted by those who cared about the boy and his progress. 'Everything's fresh for Tom at the moment,' said Sir Steve Redgrave. 'The world's media is starting to track him down and that's positive for him and the sport, but it can be negative too if you start believing your own hype. It's not an issue between now and Beijing, but it will need to be monitored through to London in 2012.'

Andy Banks was always monitoring all the dimensions of Tom's development, and was encouraged to observe a new maturity in Tom. Speaking of some difficult, testing moments that Tom had recently encountered in the sport, his coach noted with admiration that there had been no 'tears' or 'toys going out of the pram'. Instead, Tom had merely drawn more focus and determination from his soul. 'He knows he's got an extraordinary talent and he's enjoying it,' said Banks. 'But the great thing is that the confidence of the whole team has gone up. There's a massive feel-good factor in British diving at the moment. Tom has helped to lift the whole spirit.' Banks added that where he had once been required to push Tom forward at times, of late the challenge had been to hold him back. As for Tom, he played his medal hopes down. 'My school mates were always asking me if I was going to the Olympics,' he said. 'I'm just going to enjoy myself and have fun. Anything can happen in diving if you get the luck.'

•

Sadly, Tom did not get the luck when it really mattered on the day of his synchro competition, alongside Blake Aldridge. The pair had a terribly disappointing day at the office. The day had started so well for Tom. He woke up to discover that he was featured on the front page of *China Daily's* Olympic supplement. Given his propensity to believe in fate and destiny, perhaps this might have swelled his hopes? At the Beijing National Aquatics Center – also known as the Water Cube – things went far from swimmingly for Tom and Blake. Although not everyone had expected them to win the 10-metre synchro – the Chinese were the favourites to do that – nobody had expected them to finish as low as eighth – and last – place. They dived reasonably through the air, but their entry to the water was often far from ideal.

The two frontrunners were, as had been expected, China in first place with Russia in hot pursuit. Things turned sour for Tom and his partner when their inward one-and-a-half somersaults with pike went badly, scoring them just 50.40 for a total of 103.2. Then came their inward three-and-a-half somersaults with tuck, which saw them drop to eighth and last place. They were a total of 17 points outside the medal places. There was still time for them to take a very decent 77.52 awarded for a reverse three-and-a-half somersaults, but by now they were right out of the medal reckoning. The Chinese pair faltered at the end of the finals but still ended up on top overall with 468.18, while Germany (450.42) took silver. Russia ended third, beating Australia to the bronze by a narrow margin.

Tom's initial verdict on the matter was positive and upbeat. It did nothing to even hint that there might be controversy to come. 'We obviously didn't dive very well, as you could probably tell. It was disappointing but it was a great experience,' he told *Sky Sports*. 'I really enjoyed myself and had so much fun out there. That is all you can ask for getting the experience of it. We prepared like a normal competition and we treated it like a normal competition. It was just the fact it wasn't our day today, we just had a bad day. We put one hundred per cent effort into every dive we did, we just didn't pull it off.'

The story could have ended there, with a sense of resignation that it just had not been Tom's day. However, in the weeks and months to come something of a firestorm would erupt around what had gone wrong for Tom and Blake in Beijing.

The first signs of discord between the two came in an interview Blake Aldridge gave to the media about the disappointing result. 'It's a synchro team, there's two of us, and that's the hard thing about it,' he said. 'Both of you have to be on your game at the same time and that just didn't happen today.' Claiming that Tom's nerves had got the better of him, Aldridge said, 'He really struggled to get through the competition. For me to get up there and try to ease him through – well, unfortunately that didn't work.'

He then turned to a disagreement they had had about a phone call he had made during the day. '[Tom] had a pop at me before the last dive, when we were sitting down. I saw my mum in the audience and I asked her to give me a call and Tom went to me, "Why are you on the phone? We're still in the competition and we've got another dive to do." That's just Thomas – he's over-nervous and that's how it was today. Thomas should not be worrying about what I'm doing, but today he was worrying about everyone and everything and that to me is really the sole reason why he didn't perform today.'

With Tom becoming the nation's poster boy, admired across Britain and beyond, Aldridge was facing a challenge to stop himself being cast as the fall guy for their failure in the synchro. Soon, the media were making harsh judgements against the older diver. Why had he not been offering Tom the benefit of his experience, rather than taking issue with him? At this point Aldridge was in his mid-twenties and some commentators thought it was surely his duty to be the mentor for Tom who was just fourteen years, two months and twenty-one days old at the time. After all, Aldridge had previously described Tom as a 'breath of fresh air'. The press seized on the fact that Blake had made a phone call between two of their dives. Daley's disapproval at this was obvious, soon that disapproval was being echoed across the media. Talk began to circulate that Blake had let Tom down.

As the story continued to roll the question was, what would the public make of this? Balanced assessments were at a premium. Many people thought Blake was to blame, only some blamed Tom, while others just dismissed the pair as both having failed. Coach Steve Foley attempted to make a more measured summary of the events, what went wrong and what could be learned for the future. 'You could tell the body language wasn't right early on,' he said. In analyzing that body language, he observed issues with both divers but he tended towards making more comments about Tom. The picture he painted was of a partnership that had no chance of success on the day. His words were firm yet fair. 'Tom was in too much of a hurry – I hate to think what his pulse rate must have been,' said Foley. 'Blake was walking round like he was carrying the world on his shoulders.'

As the competition continued, Foley felt that both divers looked more and more defeated. By the midway point he said they 'looked like they had given up' and appeared as if they 'didn't know how to get themselves going again'. Foley echoed Aldridge's account of Tom being in an uncomfortable frame of mind. 'Tom just wasn't relaxed,' he said. 'Then again, fourteen years old, first Olympics, a lot of hype – to come back down to earth is not such a bad thing. Sure, it's hard in synchro when you let your partner down because you do feel bad about it. You just have to kiss and make up.'

Looking back on the episode in a recent interview with the author, Blake Aldridge spoke emotionally about his time as Tom's partner, and how the partnership came to an end. 'It still hurts me in millions of different ways,' he says. His journey to becoming Tom's dive partner at Beijing was one of hard work and dedication, with a tragic twist. As young as eighteen months old, Aldridge remembers holidaying in America, where he used to run to the pool and jump headfirst into the water. As he grew up his talent for swimming and diving was quickly noticed and he soared up the career ladder. Aldridge competed superbly against kids a lot older than him, as Tom later would. Diving worked for him in a way that other parts of his life did not. He is dyslexic, and his needs were not catered for by his school. By the time he was eleven he was winning diving competitions across the world and he nurtured a dream to one day compete at an Olympic Games.

He tried to get a place at the 2000 and then 2004 Olympic tournaments, but did not. Further bad luck came his way when his diving partner and best friend, Gavin Brown, was killed in a hit-and-run accident. 'He was like my brother,' says Aldridge. He then had a new partner called Gareth, but they did not build a bond comparable to his previous one. It was then that Aldridge's coach first suggested a partnership with

Tom. Aldridge was well aware of Tom's ability because he had been beaten by the youngster at a National Championships event. 'I thought I had nothing to lose by trying with this Tom kid,' said Blake.

At their first session together, it did not seem that their partnership could work, remembers Blake. Then, at the end of 2007, they tried again and things went magnificently. 'Tom had got some new dives, had grown a little bit stronger and taller,' he remembers. This time, their rapport was 'impeccable' and as a partnership, it now felt 'natural'.

Far from their age difference being an issue, Aldridge found it a positive. 'I could push my experience onto him,' he says. 'Try and guide him in the right way and help him get his mind in the right place at competitions. It became a bond, in a way it is hard to put into words. It just worked. Those early months were probably the best time in my career.' Together they competed in thirteen meets and won ten medals. 'We were a threat, everybody was scared of us,' says Aldridge. 'It's a shame it came to an end so quickly.'

Aldridge is keen to state that he had put over twenty years' work into his diving before the 2008 Olympics – two decades of sacrifices, hard work and training. 'Until you've been there and you've been through the blood, sweat and tears, it's hard to imagine how wrong it is to say someone at the Olympics wasn't trying. It's just a ridiculous thing to suggest. I'd come third in the trial for the 2000 and 2004 Olympics, before I finally made it in 2008. So that's eight years of my life gone. For anyone to turn round and say I wasn't bothered in Beijing – that is so far, far, far from the truth.'

Why *did* he phone his mother between two of the dives? 'The reason I called was because I was expecting, with good reason, a medal in Beijing. That's why I was going there. We dived and by the fifth round I realized that my dream had come tumbling down in front of us. We hadn't dived to the best of our ability. Tom was normally the one who carried the points and brought the big scores in. This was the worst score we'd ever got. I was disappointed – twelve years of training and building up to an Olympics and we both didn't dive well. I was very upset and I needed to talk to someone. Usually our coaches would be on-hand for a chat but because of the security surrounding the Olympics we were left to our own devices. Tom was very nervous, and I was nervous myself. I felt quite alone, and that combined with nerves can lead you to be a bit erratic.

'So I phoned my mum. I've been through a lot of stuff with my mum since I was a young kid. My mum and dad were divorced, meaning it was just me and my mum living together as I grew up. We went through a lot of pain together and she is like my best friend. She had always been there to pick up the pieces when

I had disappointments in diving. She always knew what to say to me. So once we were at the fifth round of diving, I rang her up and said: "Can you believe what's happened here?"'

With his emotion rising, Aldridge continued the story. 'She replied: "Don't worry, darling. You're in an Olympic final, and not many people can say that they've been there – and I'm still proud of you." It was just what I needed to hear. But the next thing I know, the press are portraying it as that I didn't give a crap about the Olympics and I was just on the phone to a mate. It was nothing like that – I was in a fragile frame of mind. My whole dream had crumbled in front of me after years and years of work.'

He argues that once a competitor knows they are not going to win a medal, it makes little difference whether they finish eighth, seventh, sixth, fifth or fourth. 'I couldn't talk to Tom about how I was feeling, because he was just a kid. I felt so alone and gutted, so I phoned my mum. It had no bearing on the result.'

•

Aldridge's Olympic journey was concluded with the 10-metre synchro, but Tom still had further business in Beijing. He was back at the Water Cube for the 10-metre platform final. He started on great form and was fourth after the first round, an amazing placing for a competitor of his age and experience. His opening effort had been the back two-and-a-half somersaults with one-and-half twists with a pike, for which he scored 81.6. He was overtaken after this and ended up in seventh place. This was no disgrace at all for Tom, who had won this round at the 2008 European Championships. He had also won plenty of admirers for his performance, which had started with a cheeky grin and even a small titter from him as he walked onto the platform for his first dive of the final. After a shaky beginning to his semi-final dives it was a charismatic start from the youngster. Plenty of British athletes were in the audience, including triple gold medal-winning cyclist Chris Hoy. Prime Minister Gordon Brown was also looking on as Tom dived.

After his 81.6 opener, Tom posted 78 points for his next dive, giving him 159.6 after two rounds. However, it was a tough field and at this stage, in seventh place, he was a total of 10.5 points away from the medal reckoning. In the next round, he fell to eighth place but enjoyed a renaissance when he moved up to sixth place after his fifth dive, the three-and-a-half somersaults with tuck, for which he was awarded 84.15. Ultimately, he finished seventh when his final dive only saw him net 64.6. The winner was Australia's Matthew Mitcham who scored 112.10 in his penultimate dive to guarantee victory over Zhou Luxin of China.

After the disappointment of the synchro, Tom was smiling again. 'It was great,' he said. 'I enjoyed myself all the way through. There were some dives I did miss but I still loved every second of it. I was nervous but good nerves with lots of adrenalinee – which was good because I had done all the hard work of getting through the prelims and the semi-final. The final I was just out to enjoy myself. There were loads of Union Jacks flying in the crowd so you couldn't ask for more.'

It was clear that Tom had learned so much from his time in Beijing. His eyes were forever wide open, taking in what was going on around him in the world of diving. He looked up to those older than him in the sport (which constituted most of those involved, of course) and looked at their experiences, forever trying to learn lessons. The openly gay diver Matthew Mitcham spent a lot of time with the British team during the Olympics. Tom came to feel sad for Mitcham and what he faced because of his sexuality. 'It's terrible – he's the only Australian who can't get any sponsors, because he's gay. He jokes about it but it must be very annoying,' he said in an interview with the *Guardian*. 'Imagine winning Olympic gold and not being sponsored?' It was admirable how mature, thoughtful and observant Tom was becoming about his sport. His empathy for Mitcham's plight was also impressive, suggesting a compassionate side to Tom's nature.

Tom could fly home with his head held high. At fourteen, an Olympic medal would have been extraordinary. 'I was quite disappointed,' he said, 'but it was a great experience and I really enjoyed myself. I had so much fun out there. That's all you can ask, getting the experience.'

As soon as he arrived back home, the talk was of school and his GCSEs. He was to take nine exams, and told the *Sun* how he felt being back in the classroom, 'It's a bit strange coming back to school but it will all be normal again soon,' he said. 'It's good to dive into my books again. My favourite subject is Spanish – don't know why but I really enjoy it. It's great to see some of my friends again.'

Tom arrived back at school a fundamentally changed boy from the one who had left it prior to the Olympics Games. He was now not just an Olympic athlete – though that alone was a big enough thing to set him aside from his schoolmates – he was also now something of a celebrity. During, and either side of, the Olympic Games Tom had sparked the fascination of the British media. A poster boy for the nation, a pin-up for teenage girls and generally a guy who attracted interest, admiration and affection: he was now famous.

He was about to find out that there were both benefits and drawbacks from being in such a position.

CHAPTER SIX

•

Fame

'He has that something about him. I'm not even going
to try and define it. Let's call it an X-factor.'
LEON TAYLOR, Olympic silver medallist

TOM HAS LONG BEEN OPEN about how comfortable he
is with his fame. He enjoys much of the attention that
he has been afforded, and as he aspires to become a
television presenter in time it is of great use to him. He
regularly grants interviews to various media outlets and
from an early age, it was clear that he was at ease in
front of a camera, or with a microphone, tape recorder
or notebook near his face. Given the context of the times
in which he came to public prominence, Tom has proven
a well-timed breath of fresh air for the public, who were
tiring of celebrities whose hunger for stardom seemed
to far, far exceed their qualification for it.

Tom's fame had actually kicked off before the Olympic
countdown had truly begun. It was after his European

Championships triumph that the metaphorical spotlight first really swung the way of the lad from Plymouth. 'Since winning the European Championships there has been a lot more pressure put on top of me,' he said. 'I've just got to kind of do what I do, and enjoy myself while I'm out there. As long as I'm having fun while I'm out there, it should be fine.'

Elaborating on how his life was changing, he explained what his increased media presence meant. 'When I walk around town you get lots of people, lots of the girls pointing,' he said. 'They speak extra loud, like "Oh god! That's Tooom Daaaley!" It makes me laugh. Like, I went into Starbucks the other day and I got a free Starbucks because she recognized me. So it does have its benefits, being recognized, so it's good.'

Girls pointing at him and a coffee shop standing him a free drink – life as a celebrity was already proving agreeable to Tom. His coach Andy Banks had noticed this trend, too, and after the European Championships win he wondered if Tom could inspire new interest in the sport of diving. He told the press, 'Tom is a bit of a minor celebrity around Plymouth and maybe a few youngsters may want to try and follow in his footsteps.' Banks cautioned against Tom's rising fame prompting an accompanying rise in the level of expectations surrounding him. 'If the media are jumping on him as a possible medallist then it is wrong,' said the coach. 'And, to be fair, in my conversations with him and the media everyone is keeping the "company line" that he is going to this Olympics looking only for a performance goal.'

Tom would need to get used to the increasing demands of the press. No editor could resist the narrative of a wholesome fresh-faced boy from Devon being poised for a place at the Olympic Games. Tom did his best to take this development in his stride, but the language he uses to describe this phenomenon is telling. 'After qualification for the Olympics the press have kind of swarmed. It's been a good experience, but it's been quite hectic.' He added that his sport and the fame it was bringing him meant he had less time with his friends and family. What more could he do but attempt to look on the bright side? 'It means that I just appreciate the time I do get with them all the more,' he reasoned.

So in the aftermath of the Olympics, Tom's profile had naturally become all the higher. The press swarmed more thoroughly, the demands became more hectic. Despite his Olympic journey having been less than ideal in some senses, Tom had to contend with being a national sporting hero and a teenage heartthrob. Given that, only months earlier, he had been an essentially anonymous schoolboy from Plymouth, this was a major paradigm shift for him – and for his family, too. As Rob explained, the media interest was intense and, at times, obtrusive. 'I get phone calls every twenty minutes through the night, many from journalists or radio stations all over the world wanting to know about Tom. They don't realize the time.' Eventually, Tom and Rob would learn to adjust and devise ways to deal with the attention.

For Tom, television was proving to be the most exciting element of media attention. In 2008 he appeared on the children's television magazine show *Switch*. Among his fellow guests were the pop-rock band McFly. Tom was interviewed about his experiences at the Olympics, including being asked what sort of music he listens to. When he did not include McFly – the members of which were listening in – in his answer, the interviewer pointed out the omission. Tom laughed and said, 'Oh, and McFly – of course!'

Towards the end of the show he agreed to play a game with band member Dougie Poynter and a member of the studio audience. The game was called The Quiz of Shame. 'It's a quiz about all those things that you probably shouldn't know the answer to, but you do,' explained the presenter. The prize, it was announced to the strains of a brass fanfare, was the contents of Tom and Poynter's pockets. Among the contents of Poynter's pockets was a receipt from the fast-food restaurant Burger King. Meanwhile, Tom produced from his pockets items including a pair of swimming goggles, some tissue, a sticking plaster and a hotel room key.

As the game began, the audience member quickly

Young Tom in 2005, already a medal winner at age eleven.

And the trophies just kept coming. Tom seen here at the Mayflower Centre in Plymouth with some of his silverware.

During a training session for the British Diving Team at Ponds Forge Pool in Sheffield.

At home with dad, Rob, and mum, Debbie, in Plymouth in 2008.

Below: Tom became European Champion in Eindhoven, Netherlands, in March 2008. Still only thirteen, he was the youngest person ever to win a gold medal at the event.

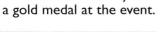

Getting ready to dive in the Men's 10m Platform Preliminary diving event at the National Aquatics Centre on Day 14 of the Beijing Olympics in August 2008.

Tom and Blake Aldridge in training for the Beijing Olympics.

Diving with Blake in the Synchronized Diving event at Beijing. It was at this event that cracks began to appear in their partnership.

At a reception held at Buckingham Palace for the 2008 Great Britain Olympic Team on 16 October 2008, Tom was very honoured to meet Her Majesty Queen Elizabeth II.

With Rob at the 2008 British Academy Television Awards, at which Tom, along with gold-medal winning heptathlete Denise Lewis, presented the BAFTA for sports coverage.

At the FINA Swimming World Championships in Rome in July and August 2009, Tom was on top form and secured the gold with three perfect 10s and three 9.5s from the judges. Despite his amazing performance, he just couldn't believe he'd really done it.

At home with mum and dad and his two brothers, Ben (centre, then aged ten) and Will (then aged thirteen).

More travelling was on the cards for Tom in 2010. In April he competed in the FINA Diving World Series in Veracruz, Mexico.

With former Olympic athlete Daley Thompson and Lord Coe on a visit to the London 2012 Olympic site.

No one could have been more proud of Tom's achievements than his beloved father, Rob, seen here welcoming his double-gold-medal-winning son back after his triumph at the Commonwealth Games in Delhi, October 2010.

In January 2011 Tom changed partners once again when he was paired with Peter Waterfield at the British National Cup Diving event in Southend (above), and (below left) celebrating after winning the Men's 10m Synchro Final during the FINA Diving World Series in Sheffield in April.

Below right: Very much the look of a champion: Tom Daley at the European Swimming Championships in Budapest, Hungary, in August 2010.

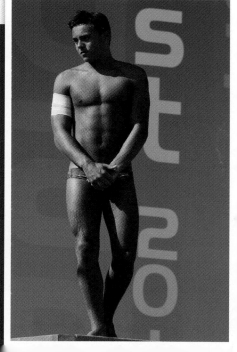

answered the first two questions. Then Tom got one right, correctly naming the youngest child of Peter Andre and Katie Price. 'Thanks for that one,' he said to someone off-camera, suggesting he had been helped. After Poynter got a Westlife-related question right, Tom was back among the points when he completed the title of the programme *Cash in the Attic*. His ever-competitive side was in evidence as he clenched his fist in celebration. However, the winner of the quiz was neither Tom nor Poynter, but the audience member.

It was a fun and polished appearance from Tom. However, the final twist in his part in the show was yet to come. At the end of the programme, McFly played their latest single *Lies* live. With its heavy brass parts and catchy guitar hooks, it quickly had the audience dancing, singing and chanting along. It is a tight, packed studio meaning that the band is literally inches away from the audience, and at the same level, rather than on a raised stage. Tom joined in with the fun by playing a sketch for the cameras during the song. In reference to the Beijing phone call controversy he pretended to phone his mother during the song, which had been a running joke throughout the show. While he was being interviewed in the studio, the host had pretended to interrupt so he could phone his own mother. For a moment, Tom had not realized it was a joke.

In another feature on BBC children's programming,

Tom was followed about by a seemingly star-struck female presenter. 'Tom Daley, diving champion and – let's face it – something of a heartthrob,' she said in her introduction. She then went up to the first diving board with Tom and admitted she felt scared. Tom agreed that it could be a scary experience, 'but you get used to it and it gets a lot easier'. She asked him about the wrist supports that he wears. 'My wrist supports are basically just to protect my wrists from bending back because if they bend back too far, you can break your wrists. You hit the water at thirty-five miles an hour so, when you're growing, you have to be cautious.' She said she had wondered if they were weights. 'No, lots of people think that,' said Tom with a giggle.

The interview then moved to the Daley household, beginning in the garage where Rob stored all his press cuttings of Tom. 'I used to open the newspaper up and think, "Oh my god, I can't believe that, that's my son in the newspaper",' said Rob. Tom then showed the interviewer the room where all his diving medals are kept, including his Olympic accreditation and the lucky monkey he had taken to Beijing. She asked how it felt sharing a room with his little brother. 'It's not too bad,' said Tom, 'because when I get home from training he's usually asleep anyway.' He added that at weekends it could be annoying when they went to sleep at the same time and Ben would ask him to leave the door ajar so light would shine in. 'That's what you've got to deal with, with little brothers, I guess.' He assured her that he got along well with his brothers most of the time, though they did have 'lots of fights as well'.

As his father was to explain elsewhere, Tom also became a celebrity in China, where divers are held in the sort of excited esteem reserved for Premiership footballers or pop legends in Britain. 'The Chinese love him,' Rob told the *Daily Mail* in 2008. 'They cheer for him almost as much as they do their own divers. They call him "Baby". There are often groupies here, teenage girls who come to watch him train. They'll sit on the balcony and watch. Then they'll wait for him outside and want a photo with him. There's a younger girl who's forever giving him a birthday card or a teddy. It's quite sweet.'

Tom's media abilities and charm were being noted again and again – even other sports people were beginning to comment as much on his confidence with the press, as on his ability as a diver. For instance, pentathlete Heather Fell told the press, 'I met up with Tom Daley, who is a really confident young man and also very accomplished with media interviews.' Another such accolade came from Leon Taylor, who said, 'There was just a glint in his eye when I talked to him.' However, it seems that Tom's eloquence is something he has developed as he has grown. One journalist I spoke with – who interviewed Tom as a nine-year-old – recalled that back then 'he could hardly hold a conversation'.

Soon, the media stories about Tom became a media story in their own right. 'Why the world focuses on Tom' ran a headline in the *Daily Mail*. The accompanying article described him as a 'man-boy' and purred with admiration at how seemingly at ease he was with the fame game and all the attention that came with it. They witnessed Tom being interviewed by channels and publications from around the world, including the prestigious American station NBC and Germany's *Stern* magazine. A Plymouth newspaper published a spread of photographs of Tom with various celebrities, including Bruce Forsyth and Piers Morgan, as well as politicians including Gordon Brown and Boris Johnson. The headline: 'Who's that with Thomas Daley?' He was the centre of attention and appeared more than comfortable being there.

Brian Viner from *The Independent* made similar observations. 'At poolside, the lad himself is taking it all in his stride,' he wrote. 'He is used to being the focus of media attention.' Indeed, even when Viner turned to some more delicate topics during his interview, he noticed that it was he, a seasoned journalist, rather than Tom, a teenaged boy, who felt most uncomfortable. 'I am painfully aware that of the two of us, I am the only one blushing', he wrote of the moment he asked Tom about girls. Viner had asked Tom a question that many men would have wondered about: would his fame through diving help him get girlfriends? 'It will help, I think,' said Tom. 'I do get lots of people coming up, and I do get lots of comments on social networking sites, Facebook and stuff. It does make it easier to get a girlfriend, I think. But I don't want a serious girlfriend before the Olympics, because I'll be away for five weeks.' Viner noted an opening Tom had left, and asked whether that meant he wanted a non-serious girlfriend. 'No,' replied Tom. 'Erm, well, no.'

A significant factor in all of this media attention was clear to the *Daily Mail*'s Ivan Speck, 'And what's more, they all came to Devon. They came in on Thursday evening and stayed over, or set off at an ungodly hour yesterday to drive to Plymouth, or even arrived bleary-eyed on the London–Penzance overnight sleeper. The point is that, for perhaps the first time, the world came to Tom.'

For Premiership football stars, it is quite normal and expected that the press will come to them. Such stars' media time is precious and their words so sought after that journalists will go anywhere to speak with them. For divers, though, and particularly for those who are still children, such willingness was less common. The fact that journalists from overseas were sufficiently interested in Tom to make such an effort for an interview was very promising for the celebrity ambitions of this 'man-boy' from Devon.

As boy increasingly became man, his appeal and fame would only swell. He became globally recognized. So much so that even such newspapers as the *Miami Herald* wrote in glowing terms of his appeal, accurately placing him as: 'Britain's answer to the Jonas Brothers – a parent-friendly safe tween-idol whose posters adorn the walls of young girls' bedrooms all over the land.'

Richard Lenton interviewed Tom for the laddish golf magazine *GolfPunk* in 2008. Reflecting back on the experience now, Lenton told me he has nothing but nice memories of his day with the thirteen-year-old Tom. 'He was my only experience of interviewing someone of that sort of age, and I wasn't quite sure what to expect,' said Lenton, an experienced interviewer and journalist on page and screen. 'He was old beyond his years in a sense, it was clear that he had been forced to grow up quickly thanks to his sport. I once taught sports journalism to a night class of teenagers, none of them were anywhere near as mature and polite as Tom. He's a smashing kid, he really is. No airs or graces to him at all, he couldn't have been more personable. I got the impression he was a very happy lad. Very articulate, too.'

Part of the feature involved trying to teach Tom, a beginner at golf, a few swings. 'I don't think he'd played golf before but he had a go at it,' said Lenton. 'He wasn't very good, to be honest. I could see how ambitious and competitive he was because when he was trying to hit the ball with his club and it went wrong, he was getting quite annoyed with himself.' (Elsewhere, Tom has acknowledged his short fuse. Asked by the *Guardian* what trait he most deplores in himself, he said, 'I have a short temper.')

Lenton has followed Daley's career since with interest and admiration. He is not shocked by Tom's progress both in sport and as a media figure. 'It didn't surprise me in the slightest, because he was so well-spoken and personable that he had many of the attributes,' said Lenton. 'The trouble is that he's still so young, so if you're looking at comparisons with, say, Sue Barker, then age is a problem. However, if he's looking to become a children's TV presenter then obviously his age is a plus point.'

In another story, Rob spoke to the *Daily Mail*, happily listing the yardsticks that charted his eldest son's ascent in fame and stature. 'The attention isn't just local,' he said. 'He's been on the BBC Sports Personality, even presenting a BAFTA. He's become a face about town. And we were at the Superstars event in London. Tom did a couple of dives and then did some judging with me. He left the judging chairs on the balcony to go to the loo. All of a sudden there were twenty or thirty girls all round him taking photographs on their phones, all wanting autographs. It took him half an hour to get back to the judging chair.'

His story was delivered with pride and also a sense of vicarious enjoyment, though he also spoke of the challenges. 'There are phone calls at three a.m. from journalists in Australia and sponsorship commitments, and he trains every day,' explained Rob. 'It's very intense . . . I'm not a pushy parent, Tom enjoys what he does and I enjoy it too. I don't coach him, we talk about normal things. When we drive home he'll ask me why a truck has got eight wheels on it, or why the cows in that field are all facing the same way.'

He spoke of the sacrifices he had made for his eldest son – and the knock-on effect they had on his life in general. For Rob, all these efforts came with a price – but also with benefits too. He weighed all this up. 'People think I must be stressed now, running around fetching Tom, looking after my other two boys. But it's happy stress. I'm not worrying about keeping a roof over our heads, my biggest worry is whether Tom will come first, second or third. My wife and I have made big sacrifices. The only time I get to myself of an evening is from nine thirty p.m. onwards, and that's before I've checked my emails or spent any time with my wife.'

As if all this attention were not enough, on 6 June 2008 Tom passed another yardstick when he travelled to London to visit Prime Minister Gordon Brown at 10 Downing Street. Later that year he attended the Royal Variety Performance, in which he introduced the *Britain's*

Got Talent winner, street dancer George Sampson, after which he had the great honour of meeting Her Majesty Queen Elizabeth II.

So, 2008 had been a fine year for Tom. 'Oh, it's been a terrific year, in sporting terms, my best yet,' he said. 'I've got lots of wonderful memories from it. The highlights were winning the gold at the European Championships and, of course, appearing in the Olympics in Beijing. I just loved the whole Olympic experience – it was fantastic. I didn't feel under any pressure. How could I when I love doing what I'm doing? I'm getting used to the media thing, although it's still very weird to be stared at by people you don't know and spoken to like they know you. So yes, it's weird, but great at the same time.'

Tom was not in any mood to rest on his laurels, indeed as far as he was concerned, the best was yet to come. Tom has the ultra-competitive tendency to always be looking forward, and to be ever of the belief that he could do better. 'Well, I've still got to train hard and concentrate on the British Championships in February,' he said. 'I want to qualify for the World Championships later in the summer, so I'll need to do well there. And next year there's the Commonwealth Games in India – I was too young to compete in Australia in 2006, although I went to those games.'

Looking ahead to 2012, Tom said that he hoped he would avoid burning out before the proceedings started.

Key to this, he explained, was that he did not grow too tall. 'If you're really tall it makes the somersaults harder because you spin slower,' he said, adding that he hoped to remain at an average height. 'It's kind of weird,' he said. 'It's kind of hard to imagine people doing that.'

Normally, Tom's narrative of the future went no further than the 2012 Olympics. This was understandable. The event was still years away, and it had for a long time represented a sense of destiny for Tom. Why should a lad in his early teens look further than three or four years ahead? But here is where Tom differed from most lads in their early teens – he was beginning to look further ahead, to the next Olympics *after* 2012. 'If I stay fit, the games in 2016 and possibly the next Olympics, too,' he said. 'I'd really like to try for those.' With him even eyeing a place in the 2020 Olympic Games, one understands why he has made so many sacrifices. He will be twenty-six by the time that tournament comes round and it would be his fifth Olympics tournament if all goes to plan. Could it be an option for Tom?

CHAPTER SEVEN

●

'We'll Break Your Legs'

'Tom's extremely high profile has led to a minority of
students acting in an immature way towards him.'
KATRINA BOROWSKI, principal of Eggbuckland
Community College

IN THE MEANTIME, Tom was beginning to face some
of the negative by-products that come with fame.
Going back to Eggbuckland Community College to
start Year 10 in September 2008, Tom was a changed
boy. He was now an Olympic diver and a national
celebrity. Young girls across the country had elevated
him to heartthrob status. Newspapers, magazines and
television channels had devoted attention to him. Even
a simple trip to the shops became more complicated,
because he would often be mobbed in the street: 'He
was waiting outside one shop and a group of teenagers
wanted to take him off for a milkshake,' remembered
his mother.

For Tom, this was basically a welcome development. He had always wanted to be famous. For some of his fellow pupils, though, this was enough to make them extremely jealous and hostile. As soon as he got back to school, Tom noticed a difference in the attitude of some of his fellow pupils.

With the benefit of hindsight, it is heartbreaking to read the first words he said publicly when he returned to education. 'I'm hoping people at school will be nice and say "well done" but there will probably be a few that will be horrible to me,' he said. Certainly, the initial reaction was one of excitement. One school friend said: 'Some people are treating him like he's a massive celebrity. You'd have thought Paris Hilton had just walked into the room. I've even seen kids in school asking for his autograph.'

Tom, meanwhile, reverted to speaking in the third person when discussing what happened next. 'Since coming back from the Olympics, you did get lots of name-calling,' he told BBC *Switch*. 'I thought I was going to get it after the Olympics and I thought it would get so bad and then drop away. But since the Olympics it has got more and more and more.' Another feature of Tom's discussion of the bullying he faced is that he often contradicts himself, at once painting it as a big issue that upset him, and then as a minor issue that was of little consequence. 'I'm just starting to get really annoyed with it now,' he continued. 'It's, like, something that doesn't really bother me, but it's just getting really annoying now. It's, like . . . you do something that you love doing and then you get the mickey taken out of you when you go to school.'

He added that the bullying was not of a particularly violent nature, but also said that as the name-calling continued, he noticed that more and more kids joined in with it. He said he found it 'immature' of them to behave in this way, and painted a picture of the problem being very widespread. However, at the conclusion of the interview he explained that he was going to continue diving, and that 'a few people at school' were never going to change that.

It was hard to gauge the scale of the problem, hard for those watching to get any sort of grasp on just how serious a problem it was. Obviously, bullying is odious at every level; there is no degree of bullying that is in any way acceptable, however small. He described the bullying, which included such things as 'name-calling, someone chucking a bit of paper at you, tipping your pencil case out'. However, any hopes that the problem was minor were dashed when it was revealed that the problem had escalated from name-calling to something far more sinister.

Within months of the problem starting, Tom encountered one of the most frightening experiences of his life as the potential scale of the bullying became terrifyingly plain. On this fateful day, an older boy and some hangers-on at school cornered Tom and issued the most spine chilling of threats: 'How much are those legs worth?' the bully asked Tom. 'We're going to break your legs.'

Tom was not just terrified, he was appalled. Such unpleasant behaviour was outside the realm of understanding for a kind, well-raised boy such as him. When he relayed news of what had happened to his family, Rob decided that enough was enough. He was no longer willing to tolerate his son being treated this way. He had lost faith that it would be dealt with by others and decided to tell the world what his son was having to face at school.

As he laid bare what had been going on, it made for painful reading. 'The bullying is severe,' he told *The Times* in an emotional interview. 'He has been tackled to the floor walking through the school field and in class they throw pens and pencils at him. Some have even threatened to break his legs. That was the last straw. The school has had plenty of opportunities to sort it out but it hasn't been done. It's gone way beyond mickey-taking; he has the whole school on his back and he knows that if he retaliates he will be all over the papers. It's just jealousy – it can't be anything else. I've been to see Tom's head of year and also the principal, because Tom has been so upset.'

The cat was out of the bag, no longer would the Daleys stand by in the hope that the bullying would prove to be a passing trend. 'I ignored the "diver boy" or "Speedo boy" comments when I came back from Beijing last year, hoping they would get fed up and stop,' Tom said. 'The trouble is they haven't, and it's even the younger kids who are joining in.'

Like many others who have experienced bullying at school, Tom responded by retreating both emotionally and physically. Once a fairly gregarious boy, he instead learned to dread the parts of the school day in which children would congregate. 'It's getting to the stage now where I think "Oh, to hell with it. I don't want to go back to school",' he said. 'I try not to go out during breaks if I can help it. I just stay in class.'

This was clearly intolerable. Tom raged at the injustice of it all. Why, he asked himself, did he have to face this nasty treatment merely because he had managed to make a success of doing something he loved? He was getting a crash-course in the jealousy and brutality that bubbles under the surface for some people. He might have ended up feeling quite alone, if it were not for the support of his family and of a small but significant group of pals he had found at school. 'I'm lucky I've got four good friends,' he said. 'They either sit in class with me or we try and find a far-off corner of the field where no one can see us.'

While these friends proved an enormous help to Tom, it was only of limited and temporary nature. Hiding in the corner of the playground was not something that could work forever, nor would anyone want it to. Tom quickly appreciated the irony of his position. In the country at large he was more known and liked than he had ever been. Once he stepped inside the school gates, the opposite was true. Never had he felt less popular and isolated. There was no hiding the hurt he felt and he summed it up with eloquent sadness: 'I have fans outside school, but in school, it's the opposite – they all hate me.' What made it particularly hard to deal with was that he 'didn't really understand' what prompted the bullying. Acutely aware that he was not the only schoolchild facing bullying, Tom used his position to reach out to other kids facing the problem. 'You're not alone,' he told them in one interview.

Katrina Borowski, principal of the school, was forced to respond to the growing media profile that the Daley bullying saga was attracting. 'Tom's extremely high profile has led to a minority of students acting in an immature way towards him,' she said. 'All involved in his education are supporting him as best we can and immediate action was taken to address concerns raised.'

Rob told a local television show that there was a fear that Tom could become physically injured if the bullying took a violent dimension. Increasingly, he became of the opinion that Tom's educational future might have to lie elsewhere. 'I'll have to pull him out of school and switch to another if it continues,' Rob said. 'He should be a positive role model instead of enduring what he's had to.' Not that Rob was in any way being over-protective. He had long told Tom that he would have to expect and deal with the name-calling and teasing that his fame would prompt in school. Knowing that the corridors of any school can be unforgiving places, he advised Tom to simply let such behaviour go over his head. For the most part, Tom did just that.

Eventually, the decision was taken to remove Tom from the school. Rob quickly earmarked the place he wanted Tom to move to: Plymouth College, an establishment which, he said, 'understands the requirements of elite athletes'. The college has around 550 pupils, of whom 120 are boarders. Rob strongly encouraged Tom to move there, but was careful not to apply an inappropriate level of pressure. 'If Tom likes what he sees he'll start there immediately,' Rob said. 'I'll certainly be steering him in that direction, but I'll make sure he's happy before a final decision is made.'

Key to the appeal of Plymouth College from Rob's

perspective was that it was a place in which his son would not stand out so much. Although he knew Tom was keen and ambitious, he knew that a quieter life while at school was desirable for his son. The headmaster of the college, Dr Simon Wormleighton, promised that this could be the case. 'Tom is a special young man but he could achieve more anonymity here than at another school,' he said, as the wooing began in earnest. He continued: 'We have very dedicated young people who have all the pressures of the international spotlight but at school are able to be normal pupils and are able to follow an academic programme to get the results that they will need for the rest of their lives.'

Meanwhile, another offer came the family's way. Sussex's Brighton College offered Tom a full scholarship. 'Tom is just the sort of young person we welcome here and I am confident he would fit in very well with the other pupils,' Richard Cairns, the headmaster said. 'He would be very happy here and would be able to continue his sports career without the unnecessary added pressure of nasty bullies.'

This was a generous offer, not least since the scholarship would be to a school that normally charged £25,000 a year. However, Rob quickly decided that it was out of the question for Tom, due to the distance from home.

But the fact remained that Tom had to leave Eggbuckland – and this could have become a public relations disaster for the school. A previously unknown educational establishment was being thrust into the public eye purely as the alleged scene of the bullying of a national sporting idol and popular kid. Katrina Borowski, principal of Eggbuckland Community College, told the BBC: 'We are very sorry that Tom is leaving our college and wish him every success in his education, his diving and for the future.'

Once it was clear that Tom was leaving, Rob issued a parting shot to Eggbuckland, saying that since he and his son had spoken publicly about the bullying, they had found out that he was not alone in facing such unpleasant behaviour. 'It seems it's quite widespread, and not much is being done about it,' said Rob. However, the head of Eggbuckland insisted that the establishment does take bullying seriously and acts on it. 'We take the well being of our students extremely seriously and have a very clear policy for dealing swiftly and firmly with any incidents,' she said.

The media was watching and was firmly on Tom's side. Deborah Orr, columnist for *The Independent*, was not impressed. She spoke of a national need for more decisive action against bullying, and said the sort of approach hinted at by Eggbuckland was 'quite patently elaborate nonsense'. Successful businesswoman and *Apprentice* star Karren Brady also weighed in. She turned angrily on the bullies and Eggbuckland in her column for the *Birmingham Mail*, describing the principal's public statement as 'PC speak', and said of the assurances therein, 'That just isn't good enough'. She reserved her harshest words for the bullies themselves: 'It is the no-hopers and born losers making his life hell – his word – that need help. They can't or won't see it is achievement, not envy or creating fear that is rewarded in the wider world. I doubt they will be happy grownups.'

There was also plenty of support among the general public for Tom as he faced up to the bullies. Plymouth resident Shirley Rogers sent a letter to the *Plymouth Herald*, in which she wrote: 'These students should be proud of Tom going to the same school, and his achievements.' She also wrote movingly of the evening when she had encountered Tom at a charity evening for a local girl, before concluding: 'We say: you go, Tom, and do the best you can. There are hundreds of Plymouthians, young and old, behind you. We wish you well every step of the way. We are proud of you.' Another correspondent, J.H.A. Roberts, wrote: 'I wish these bullies could be made to go on the top board.'

Ultimately, Tom had a decision to make. He opted to follow Rob's advice and moved to Plymouth College, enrolling in June 2009 after being given what was described as a 'substantial scholarship' to attend the £4,000-a-term fees school. He left Eggbuckland at half-term, and, having spent the half-term break in Florida, he returned and joined Plymouth College. This was exciting for him in many ways. Not only did it mean he would hopefully see the back of the petty resentments and bullying that so blighted his experience at his last school, it also meant he was joining an establishment more geared up for a sporting pupil such as he, with all the commitments and other peculiarities that entailed.

'I'm really looking forward to going to Plymouth College and being with other young people who understand the pressures of high-level competition,' Tom told the *Plymouth Herald*. 'The school has a lot of experience in putting together academic programmes for pupils like me so I won't miss out on my school work when I'm away.'

For Debbie, the move was something of a shock. 'I never imagined any of my children would have a private education,' said Debbie. 'But the truth is, a better class of people send their kids there, and the youngsters who come out are the top doctors and lawyers of the future.'

Plymouth College headmaster Dr Simon Wormleighton publicly welcomed Tom to the school, and spoke of his delight that he was joining the ranks. He expanded on why Plymouth College was an appropriate place for Tom to study. 'In common with many of our athletes, he has a busy training and competition schedule so we are working on a flexible academic programme to fit in with his various commitments. We will help Tom to keep on top of his studies so he can reach the high academic standards of which he is capable while fulfilling his extraordinary potential in the pool.'

The facts backed up Tom and his new headmaster's optimism. Plymouth College has a deserved reputation, and runs an elite programme of over thirty national and international swimmers. One former pupil is Cassie Patten, an open-water swimmer who grabbed a bronze medal at the Beijing Olympics. She won a host of world, European and national medals during her four years at the school. 'But the school's sporting headlines are not just limited to swimming,' added a spokesman. 'The Plymouth College modern pentathlon and fencing academy saw its first British champion last year and boasts an England U-18 fencer. In addition, a fourteen-year-old gymnast won silver and bronze medals in the 2008 British Gymnastic Championships and an U-19 England cricketer will take up a professional contract with Somerset this summer.'

•

That might have been that, with regard to the bullying. However, this has become a firm part of the Daley narrative, often referred to when Tom is profiled and discussed. More recently, Daley and his team have tried to put a slightly different spin on what happened to him. During a key interview with the *Guardian*'s Weekend supplement in October 2010, Tom, his father, and a PR representative from Tom's sports management company, had an interesting exchange and a difference of opinion. The journalist, Decca Aitkenhead, reflected afterwards that had she not have raised the subject of the bullying Tom suffered, she is 'almost certain' that Tom would not have done so himself.

However, she did raise it and was told by Tom, 'It wasn't anything major – I never really understood why it happened.' She described Tom's tone as he spoke about this as 'mild'. No sooner had Tom answered her question than the PR intervened to try and play the issue down. 'I think it was normal teenage kids' stuff,' said the PR. 'It's been blown out of all proportion by the media.'

The issue becomes ever more mysterious and the accounts of it are contradictory. If Tom was being targeted to the extent that he was having things thrown at him during lessons and bullies were threatening to break his legs, then that would constitute more than 'normal teenage kids' stuff'. Likewise, if a small group of children were originally behind the bullying but that then escalated, according to Tom, into a larger group, including younger children, targeting him, then that too would be beyond 'normal'.

Indeed, if what Tom was facing really had been just 'everyday stuff' then his family would not have decided to move him from one school to another. Rob was at Tom's side as he gave this interview. He got involved in the discussion at this point, saying that moving schools was 'the best thing that had ever happened' to his son. More confusion came when Aitkenhead asked whether Tom's previous school had been supportive of him during the bullying he faced. Simultaneously, Tom said that they *had* and his father said that they had *not*. Following this, Tom said, 'Yeah, they were.' But his father gave him what Aitkenhead described as 'a dark look' and said 'I don't think so – if they were you would still be there, wouldn't you?'

Again, the PR intervened and told Rob that this was an interview with Tom, not him. Rob backed away, apologizing and saying, 'I'm not allowed to talk.' (Though it seemed the PR was allowed to!) Tom laughed and said 'Yeah, he is [allowed to talk], he's just being an idiot.' He then insisted again that the school had been 'very supportive'. Aitkenhead recorded that Rob then 'pulled a face' that suggested he still believed otherwise.

There were mixed messages emerging on this delicate topic. It was then left to Tom to try and reconcile these differences of opinion, and contradictory messages, into something unified. 'The only reason it got bad was just cos the media blew it out of all proportion,' he said. 'And then there wasn't anything I could do cos the people at school would see it in the newspapers and think they were getting to me, that kind of thing. That made it a little bit worse. But the new school's completely different, it's full of young people who understand about training and everything. And the good thing is, I still see all of my friends from my old school. I still meet up with them at least once a week.'

The fact that Tom and Rob took the trouble to highlight and publicize the problem was important. It would have been easy to quietly move schools and save Tom the embarrassment of the issue being made public. Drawing attention to what was happening to him meant that other children who were subjected to bullying were given comfort and encouragement. One of the feelings that many bullying victims admit to is that they feel alone. To see a high-profile youngster like Tom speaking out against and overcoming bullying, offered them some comfort in their darkest hours. Also, the fact that a robust athlete and nationally popular teen such as Tom was identified in the public imagination as the victim of bullying was significant. For so long victims of bullying have been identified in the public mind as quiet, introspective children. The truth is that all kinds of people are bullied, and often it is because of their popularity or positive, attractive qualities that people face such treatment.

Tom's experiences prompted others to come forward. Another diving star, Leon Taylor, who had won a silver medal for Britain, said: 'I was actually bullied at school as well. It's not uncommon when you get a lot of attention from outside for kids to do that.' He promised to offer what support he could to Tom. 'There can be a lot of jibes, and kids can say some horrible things. I'll be touching base with Tom as soon as I can to discuss it with him.'

Boxer Joe Calzaghe, too, offered the benefit of his own experiences. 'Bullying is a horrible thing to go through – I know because it happened to me,' he told the *Sun*. 'It needs to be dealt with because it can lead to self-harming, even suicide. Maybe if they had someone to talk to then this wouldn't happen.' There was even speculation that Tom's former dive partner Blake Aldridge had been targeted due to the fame his diving had brought him when he was beaten up at a Southampton nightclub.

A past in which one has been bullied is no barrier to future success, though – ask Bill Clinton, Miley Cyrus,

Tiger Woods and Robert Pattinson – all of whom were unpleasantly targeted as kids and all of whom rose to the very top of their respective professions. The list goes on and on, from Hollywood superstar Tom Cruise to singer Christina Aguilera, countless celebrities have an unhappy chapter of bullying in their past. Many of them use the taunts of the cruel kids to spur them on to higher things.

So, what became of the pupils back at Eggbuckland who had been so unpleasant to Tom? Katrina Borowski told the *Guardian* that 'certain students have been sanctioned' as a result of their behaviour towards Tom. With that statement their place in the limelight – albeit anonymously – came to an abrupt end. Tom, meanwhile, has not so much risen, as soared above the lot of them. As yet more medals are added to the collection, Tom continues to become more successful and popular, the bullies are long forgotten.

There can be no finer response than that.

CHAPTER EIGHT

•

Champion of the World

'I represent Tom Daley, I'm Tom's dad . . . Tom, can
you come and give me a cuddle?'
ROB DALEY

BY THE SPRING OF 2009, although facing many difficulties,
Tom managed to keep focusing on what mattered most
to him: his diving. At the third round of the World Cup, at
Ponds Forge in Sheffield, he overcame a nagging problem
with his back to pull off a breathtaking performance. In
the week prior to the competition he had needed fairly
intensive work on his back, yet no spectators could
have guessed this as they watched him soar to a silver
medal in the final of the 10-metre platform. It had been
a challenging qualifying pool at Ponds Forge. The line-
up for the final was, naturally, even tougher. It included
two Olympic champions and the new kid on the block
from China, the extraordinarily promising Qiu Bo, the

reigning world junior champion. With so much on his mind – including the ongoing bullying issue, injury *and* his father's illness – how could young Tom excel over his six dives among such sublime opponents?

Yet, somehow, Tom summoned the strength and focus to put in what many considered the performance of his life. Statistically this was certainly the case – his 540.85 points was a personal best. This put him ahead of the aforementioned Qiu Bo and the Australian Olympic champion and Olympic gold medal winner Matthew Mitchum and behind Chinese synchro gold medallist Huo Liang.

Tom was notably robust and aggressive in his approach to the six dives. He seemed more pumped up and determined than ever. Having noted a tendency to under-perform in the final dive of a series at past events, he put his all into the sixth and final dive in Sheffield. He studied the scoreboard carefully before the sixth dive. This gave him an acute understanding of what was required – what he had to do to win – as well as an added motivation to finish on a high, rather than a low.

No wonder he felt pumped up following the event. 'I enjoyed the pressure this time, I became more aggressive and really went for the last dive,' he said afterwards, acknowledging the tactic. 'If you had told me before a final with two reigning platform Olympic champions and a Chinese diver I have never beaten as a junior that I would win a silver medal, I would never have believed it.'

However, due to concerns about his back and problems obtaining a visa for him, Tom decided not to travel to Mexico for the final round of the World Cup. Instead, he decided to go to Florida to attend a training camp.

Among those who had watched him in Sheffield was Team GB's newly appointed performance director, Alexei Evangulov. This was a man who knew his stuff – having guided Russia to five diving medals at the Olympics in Beijing. Evangulov was encouraged and impressed by Tom's performance, and singled him out for special praise afterwards. 'Thomas Daley is a diving genius,' he said. 'I already knew that from my time when I used to study him as an opposition coach. I know that in the world there are not so many like him.'

This sense that Tom is special is hard to deny. Soon, he would be the envy of many males of *all* ages when he was photographed for the iconic *Vogue* magazine alongside none other than supermodel Kate Moss. Ever the ambitious and canny operator, Tom was not to be satisfied by merely being photographed alongside one of the world's most famous females. Instead, he went one better and asked a favour of Moss, as we shall see. It should have been a big ask, one that most people would be far too scared to even consider, let alone actually suggest out loud.

First, though, came the photo-shoot where Tom met Kate, photographed by Bruce Weber. Mr Weber is an American fashion photographer of fine repute. As well as snapping for *Vogue*, he has worked for a huge range of other magazines including *GQ, Vanity Fair, Elle, Life, Interview*, and *Rolling Stone*. He has also worked in film, directing promotional videos for various pop acts, including the Pet Shop Boys. He has even created his own fashion label. Being photographed by him is in itself an honour in any star's life. The fact that Tom was being snapped alongside supermodel Kate Moss made it all the more exciting.

The *Vogue* photographs were taken for a series called 'London in Love'. Other models were featured in the series, including male stunner Harry Goodwins. Tom and Kate looked absolutely great in the shots, which were taken in a moody 1950s sepia style at a swimming pool. In one, both are seen in the pool playfully nibbling a thumb while looking with a cheeky yet vulnerable expression at the camera. More playful yet was the one in which Tom is splashing Moss. He looks more amused than her, though she is obviously taking it in good humour. The most striking of the set sees Moss leaning erotically against a door with 'Male Changing Room' emblazoned on it. Tom stands a little to the side with his fists clenched and a look of disbelieving triumph on his face.

In other memorable snaps, there was one of Tom alone, smiling and holding his fingers in a 'v for victory' position. Another featured Tom and Moss outside of the pool and glaring into the camera. Tom has an Adidas towel wrapped round his waist, and a 'hoody' pulled up over his head. Moss stands next to him, pulling off the sort of smouldering pout that made her one of the world's most famous models. It was a fascinating, if surprising photo-set.

What happened next was certainly very unexpected. Tom has a growing interest in photography, which he has often described as a 'relaxing' pastime. He was studying it at school and had a project on his mind. With one of the world's most photographed women at his side during the *Vogue* shoot, he decided to ask her for some help.

Tom describes how he broached the topic with typical understatement – as if this sort of thing happened all the time. 'I asked Kate if she would be kind enough to model for a particular shot I wanted, one inspired by an original portrait by David Hockney,' he said. Luckily, Ms Moss who normally charges mega-bucks to be photographed, was in agreeable mood. 'I told her it was for part of my course and she agreed,' said Tom. Most boys of Tom's age would never think of asking such a question had they been in his shoes, even fewer would actually have done so.

Was Tom rather taken by Kate, as many lads of his age would be? When Tom was asked about girlfriends by a *Daily Telegraph* interviewer, his response was brief and somewhat vague. 'If I did have a girlfriend, she'd have to understand that diving is my main priority,' he said. Again, he shrugged the matter off with a brief, non-committal response. Indeed, he was keen to play down the idea that his lifestyle was particularly racy. 'People looking at me in competition might think it's an easy, glamorous life,' he said. 'Trust me, it's far from that.'

•

There can be no doubt how hard Tom works on his fitness and form, but between all the diving and intensive training and preparation, there *are* moments of glamour. For instance, in April 2008, he not only attended the glamorous BAFTAs at the London Palladium, he even presented one of the awards. Prior to his arrival on the stage, Joanna Page and Rob Brydon from the BBC comedy *Gavin & Stacey* had presented the Best Comedy gong to Kayvan Novak, for the *Fonejacker* series. Meanwhile, Tom waited nervously backstage with Olympian Denise Lewis, who would co-present the Sports Coverage award with him. They announced the nominees, which included the Wimbledon Men's Final 2006, the Boat Race and the Rugby World Cup 2007

Semi-Final. However, the winner was ITV's Formula 1 Canadian Grand Prix coverage. No sooner had Tom and Denise Lewis handed over the award than their time on the stage was up. As always happens at events such as this, after months of looking forward to it, the action for each individual participant was over very quickly. Still, to have presented a BAFTA at just thirteen was a big deal for Tom. Not many people can say they have done that.

Although always at pains to emphasize that he had earned the rarefied position he finds himself in, Tom was also keen to paint himself as, in some ways at least, a normal British teenage boy. 'I've been working my socks off since I was seven. Even if it is hard some days, and sometimes you might dip if you are tired, I really enjoy it. Anyway, I do have Saturday afternoons and Sundays off when I can do normal things for a fifteen-year-old, like going to the cinema or watching *X-Factor*.' His image as a down-to-earth teenager is corroborated by many who have met him. As we have seen, many journalists met Tom around this time. Despite their concerns that they might be about to encounter a young brat, they were positive about the person they found. 'My fears of encountering a precocious kid with extraordinary talent who'd been spoilt rotten by premature fame were unfounded,' wrote Richard Lenton in *GolfPunk* magazine after meeting Tom that time at a golf course. 'Tom Daley is as nice a lad as you'd wish to meet.'

Looking forward, those closest to Tom were sure that his success and fame would not change him or make him any kind of show-business brat. The Daleys are a grounded and grounding family. Just let anyone in their number try to get too big for their boots, and the rest of the family would have soon cut them down to size. So with the Commonwealth Games coming up in 2010 and then London 2012 ahead of Tom, it was safe to assume that his feet remained on the ground, when they were not on the diving platform. 'He's certainly not a prima donna,' said Rob resolutely. 'I can't see that changing. He's been experiencing it from so young that if it was going to change him, it would have done so already.'

For Tom, welcome though his increasing fame was, success in diving continued to be his driving force. In April 2009, Tom triumphantly retained his British individual 10-metre platform diving crown. His joy was tempered by the fact that he had been prevented from also competing in the synchro pairs event because his diving partner, Blake Aldridge, was unavailable. Aldridge was recovering from injuries he had sustained during an attack on him in a nightclub in Southampton.

As far as Rob was concerned, this put an end to any hope of resurrecting the Daley–Aldridge partnership. After the controversy of Beijing and then the nightclub story, Rob had lost patience. 'I do not want him to dive with Blake anymore,' said Rob. 'In six months' time Tom will have a different partner.' Tom said of the nightclub incident: 'That sealed it, you almost don't want to be associated with him when that happens.'

However, not everyone agreed that the matter was that straightforward. A spokesman for British Swimming explained that it was up to Tom and his coaching team to choose his partner. The spokesman also said: 'Tom wished Blake all the best in his recovery last week and the feeling is that the pair will be diving again later in the year. Certainly, speaking to Andy Banks and Tom on Friday, they want to get back together.'

Aldridge, meanwhile, took this rejection hard. 'The nightclub incident wasn't my fault, I was attacked by three guys,' he told me. He was left with a large scar on his face, and a broken nose. Worse was to come. 'Next thing I know, Tom's Dad turned round and said: "Well, this is the end of Blake's partnership with Tom – he's burned his bridges now." It was very demoralizing. I wondered how they could be so unsympathetic. But that's life, you just have to pick up the pieces and move on. That's what I'm trying to do.'

In the end, Rob won the day, and soon the Daley–Aldridge partnership was consigned to history. 'As a parent, we have a duty to look after our kids, make sure everything goes right for them, goes as smooth as possible,' Rob told the BBC.

He continued to support Tom as best he could,

wherever he went. In May, Tom took his first title of 2009 in the men's 10-metre platform at the FINA Grand Prix in Fort Lauderdale, Florida. It was his penultimate dive that swung it, a backward three-and-a-half somersaults tuck which earned him straight 10s from all the judges. He was proud of his winning score of 554.90, which came against strong opposition from Olympic silver medallist Zhou Luxin, and 2008's World Cup champion, Sascha Klein. The Great Britain team had already landed three silver medals in Florida – one of which went to Tom and partner Max Brick in the synchronized event – when, three days later, Tom proudly added a gold to the UK haul.

•

It was in July 2009 that Rob first joined his son in the public spotlight, when he followed Tom to the 13th FINA World Swimming Championships in Rome. It was an eventful trip for many reasons. By the time father and son returned to their Plymouth home, Rob had become a national figure himself. It was an uncomfortable entrée for Rob – both in the execution of it at the time, and in the sense of the questions and suggestions it prompted.

In reality, few people expected Tom to be among the medal winners in Rome. He was up against some extremely talented opponents, and he also had a relatively low tariff – the degree of difficulty of his dives – in comparison to the other competitors. Therefore there was plenty of reason to be cautious of his chances, as Tom was only too aware. 'It is going to be very, very tough to get a medal because my tariff is lower than all the other divers,' he said. 'After the World Championships I'll be working on some new dives to get my tariff up. But for now all the other divers will obviously have higher tariffs so I have to hope they make some mistakes. The thing I have to do is dive at my very best and put the pressure on them so that maybe they make those mistakes and I can take advantage.'

These now seem strangely prophetic words, given what transpired, as Tom competed in the 10-metre platform final. It was a sunny day at the open-air venue. Tom looked tanned and composed as he prepared for his first dive. The fact he was diving at an outdoor pool was another significant factor for Tom. 'It is very different diving outdoors than indoors,' he had said. 'It is hard to know exactly where you are and which way you are facing because the sky is the same colour as the water.'

A television commentator who had just spent three-quarters of an hour with Tom just before the event said, 'He seemed pretty calm, he seemed relaxed.' As Tom entered the sixth round of the 10-metre platform final he was in third place. There seemed precious little prospect of him finishing any higher than that. Indeed, for him to even come third would have been a very impressive feat. After all, he was up against a strong pack including the favourite, Qiu Bo, and the Australian Olympic gold medallist Matt Mitcham. Few expected young Tom to be able to compete with them. However, towards the end of the competition, he suddenly upped his game, while simultaneously his rivals crumbled. The crowning glory came when Tom scored 100.30 for his final dive.

What an exciting competition it had been, with a real grandstand finish. Tom had kept in touch with the frontrunners with his first four dives. On the final dive, it was Zhou Luxin who went first and he set the bar very high indeed when he scored 100.70. Tom went next and scored three perfect 10s and three 9.5s for a 100.30 total.

'Yeeeeees,' screamed the BBC television commentator. 'Come on, Tom! What a dive, what a dive, what a dive! You're looking at Great Britain's first medallist in a World Championships at diving.'

Tom's smile when he saw the final scoring was enough to melt any heart. Andy Banks ran up and patted his young diver on the back. He had indeed done well but he knew that the next two main contenders would both need to fluff their respective final dives for him to win. What, he must have thought, were the chances of that happening? So imagine his excitement as he stood by the pool and watched first Mitcham and then Qiu both mess up their final dives. Qiu made his mistake with his entry into the water, and suffered a 79.80 final score.

It had been a tense finish, but Tom was world champion. He looked stunned as he approached the podium. However, when it came time for him to literally step onto the top step he did so with grace. He looked every inch the champion – albeit a slightly young and fresh-faced one.

He bent his neck to take the medal, shook the hand of the medal-presenter. A lady then presented him with a cuddly toy and some flowers. He kissed her on both cheeks. As he waved to the crowd and enjoyed the acclaim, Tom must have felt on top of the world – for as world champion that was exactly where he was.

Speaking afterwards, Tom confirmed that he genuinely did not expect to be among the medal winners, and certainly had not anticipated finishing at the top of the podium. 'Getting into the final, I just thought, "Go out there and do your best and see what happens". I thought I was going to come fourth and I would have been really happy with that. But then to come away with a medal was going to be great, then a gold medal was just insane.'

Of the dramatic, final two rounds, Tom said: 'Those two are my favourite dives and that is why I leave them until last because I know under pressure I can do them well. I really thought they were going to catch up because they only needed seven-and-a-halves and eights and for them not to get it is just crazy.' Ever one to look at the bigger picture, he said: 'Hopefully this will put British diving on the map . . . Hopefully it will help everyone diving to get a bit more publicity.'

Meanwhile, his proud father Rob had been beyond excited as he watched Tom. 'It was a brilliant feeling when he was fourth,' he said. Then when he got bronze it was amazing. When he got silver I thought "don't let it stop". Then waiting for the last score for the Chinese diver seemed to take an eternity. I had a flashback of his whole life and I looked up and he was world champion – and he is fifteen! It is an unbelievable feeling.' Shock and pride all round, it had been an amazing day for the Daley family.

Tom had another challenge to overcome in the press conference after the event. This conference has since gone down in legend thanks to an unexpected intervention made by Tom's father. Rob was bursting with pride, excitement and emotion. Despite not being an accredited journalist – and looking every bit the interloper, thanks to the small plastic Union flag he was boyishly holding in his right hand – he managed to get into the press conference. As the discussion was opened to questions from the floor, Rob put up his hand to ask one, just as any journalist would. Tom had already spotted Rob and later remembered noting at the time that he seemed in something of an emotional mood. 'I could just see him at the back, I could see him starting to cry, and I was like "Oh Dad . . . what are you *doing*?"'

Rob was handed the microphone. 'I represent Tom Daley, I'm Tom's dad,' he said as the cameras spun around to face him. 'Tom, can you come and give me a cuddle?' As amusement and a little confusion spread through the room, Rob added emotionally, *'Please? Come on, please! Come on!'* Tom got up sheepishly and walked across the room to Rob. 'Don't make me cry,' he said with embarrassment. They embraced as Tom giggled nervously.

A reporter asked, 'This means the world to both of you, doesn't it? How proud are you of your son?' As Rob proudly patted Tom's cheeks, he said: 'A million reasons. He's a good lad, he's a good boy isn't he?' Tom then gave credit to Rob for driving him to his training sessions each day, before adding, 'But this is slightly embarrassing.' Rob laughed and said it was not embarrassing, giving Tom another friendly pat on the head. 'Yes it is, Dad,' replied Tom, muttering, 'Oh God!' as he walked back to the front table to resume the press conference proper.

Meanwhile, an official felt the need to explain what had happened: 'I hope everyone understood that the gentleman down there was not a journalist, but – as I understand – the father of Tom Daley. Let's continue with this press conference . . .' What an extraordinary intervention it had been – at once hugely emotional, deeply touching and very awkward.

As such, the story was too much for the media to resist. Tired of mundane press conferences in which dull athletes offer anodyne, clichéd soundbites, the press made Rob's intervention the story of the day. Rob was quite unrepentant, despite Tom's discomfort and the feeling of some that he had behaved inappropriately. As far as he was concerned, he had done absolutely nothing wrong. 'The door was open, I just walked in,' he said. 'All I did was take the mike and when they asked for questions I asked a question.'

His feeling was that the circumstances were extraordinary, so his behaviour had also stepped beyond the usual. To him this seemed quite understandable. 'I am absolutely elated, you wouldn't believe how happy I am,' said Rob. 'All of the hard work has been worth it. I knew that if he had a good day and did everything right he could do it.'

Recalling the experience of watching her son become world champion, Debbie was no less excitable back home in Devon. 'I am really, really proud of him,' she said. 'It was a shock to the system, to be honest, to think that he is a world champion at the age of fifteen – and also that he is the first Briton to win it as well. I am really, really pleased. It was really unexpected.'

Rob's happiness was to be tested when some individuals made unpleasant and petty remarks about him in the wake of the press conference. Given that many young, precocious sports stars have become so successful so young as a result of extremely pushy parents, some wondered whether Rob's press conference moment was evidence of such a situation in the Daley family. This was not the only criticism made. Some also accused Rob of trying to steal some of Tom's fame, to become a celebrity himself.

The simple truth is that Rob was a proud and emotional man. Which father would not be overcome with such feelings after watching his fifteen-year-old son become a world champion? Factor in his health problems and the fact that those who have suffered from brain tumours often find their behaviour can become less inhibited and more impulsive, and you have the perfect recipe for Rob's conduct. After all the years of supporting his son and watching him develop in the sport he so loved, it is unsurprising that he felt so elated. Rob said of the snipers, 'I don't care. I'm still over the moon.' He told Tom that when he, Tom, becomes a father, he will understand the emotional forces that drove him that day.

Debbie, though, was hurt by the criticisms made of her husband. In a later interview she returned to that day and, defending Rob, tried to explain the context. 'What people were saying after the press conference was quite hurtful,' said Debbie in the interview with the *Daily Telegraph*. 'It was implied that he was hounding Tom, but that just isn't the case.' She continued, 'Robert goes to see Tom's competitions on his own because we can't afford for all of us to go. Under the rules, he's not allowed to spend any time with Tom before a competition, and in Rome he hadn't seen him for two days. Then Tom won the world title, and was whisked away, and just as Rob had given up looking for him and was heading for the airport, he poked his head in an open door and saw it was the press conference.'

Back at their Plymouth home, Rob was also the unofficial archivist for Tom's career, keeping a growing collection of press cuttings that grew so large it had to be moved into the garage. Tom's growing haul of swimming medals and trophies were also prominently displayed in the family home. Both parents were at pains to make sure the world understood that they were equally devoted and committed to all three of their boys. With William and Ben increasingly playing rugby, Rob also hopped in the car to follow their sporting fortunes. 'I always go and watch Bill and Ben play,' he said.

Tom echoed his mother's refutation that either of his parents were 'pushy'. He was keen to emphasize that they were certainly very encouraging, but he drew a distinction between that and anything more. 'My parents are really supportive,' he said. 'If anyone's been pushing it's me, because I've worked hard to achieve my goals. I know they've made sacrifices, and I'm really grateful but

I also know that if I wanted to give up diving tomorrow, they would respect my decision.'

More than anything, Tom understood his father's emotional nature. 'There's a time and place for Dad to be emotional,' he told *The Times* newspaper. 'He does it all the time and someone always gets it on camera. I guess that's what parents do. If I win more and more, I think he won't do it as much.'

In a final amusing turn on the story, Rob revealed that after the press conference he made sure that Tom handed him the gold medal for safe-keeping. Rob was not about to let Tom just chuck it into a bag, whereupon, '[It would] come out with his towel and there'll be yoghurt on it. It'll be safe with me.' Another medal to be added to the growing collection back home in Plymouth – and this time a gold medal that confirmed Tom was a world champion.

CHAPTER NINE

●

Commonwealth Golds

'[Tom is] an inspiration to all those involved in British
sport and to young people right across the country.'
GORDON BROWN, Prime Minister

BACK HOME IN BRITAIN, Tom was becoming an ever-
more loved national figure. His victory had been
celebrated across the media, elevating the sport of
diving into far more prominence than it had ever
enjoyed previously. Newspapers cheered the win, with
the *Sun*'s memorable headline reading: 'Top Teen Tom
is 15 to Won!' The BBC went to town on the story, with
a lengthy feature on its website headlined: 'Tom Daley's
life less ordinary'. His life was indeed extraordinary
– and becoming increasingly so. The Prime Minister,
Gordon Brown, praised him as an 'inspiration to all
those involved in British sport and to young people
right across the country'.

He had also inspired other divers. Barnsley diver

Megan Sylvester was also at Rome. A few months younger than Tom, she looked up to him and was naturally excited and encouraged by his gold. 'It's made me realize that it can be done,' she said. 'It's inspired me to strive for future success.' It seemed lots of people were cheered by and were cheering for Tom – but he is that sort of person, it is difficult *not* to feel pleased for him.

Still, with his success, as the stakes rose higher and higher, Tom was certainly faced with increasing pressure. Fortunately, he was essentially at ease with this trend. 'It's something you have to cope with, pressure. I normally respond well to it,' he told the *Daily Mail*. He explained that his competitive spirit drove him onwards and upwards. 'If I see someone do a good dive, I want to do a better one,' he said. 'That's what you need to have in a competition if you want to win the gold medals.'

As with many of Tom's statements about his sport, this comment manages to combine a stating of the obvious with a good insight into his mindset. Of course, one needs the ability to be able to beat the rest of the pack, but before such ability can be harnessed effectively, the mind does need to be in the right place. As a very young diver, Tom's mind was sometimes unfocused as he went about his sporting craft. He occasionally responded to setbacks badly, with tears shed and tantrums not entirely unknown. However, as he progressed through his mid-teenage years, Tom became a more balanced and focused athlete. Now, with the competitive and ambitious urge that ran through him channelled with focus and increased maturity, Tom found himself reaping the benefits. His maturity was not about to dilute his ambition to be the best.

One of Tom's favourite songs is *The World's Greatest* by R. Kelly. The lyrics chime well with his personality. 'It is very good motivational music and I listen to it a lot when I am competing,' he told the *Daily Telegraph*. 'It makes me want to do well and train harder and make everything as good as it possibly can be with my diving. It is one of my goals to be the "world's greatest", so when I listen to this song it just makes me more determined to achieve that.'

His youthful determination was now complimented by a more adult poise. Still, he remained a teenage boy at heart – and a wholesome one at that. For instance, when he won gold in Rome, his mother was asked how Tom would celebrate. Far from imagining some sort of over-triumphant outburst, or debauched behaviour, his mother predicted, 'Perhaps he will have an ice cream! That's something he likes to do when he's had a win.' As long as he watches the calories, a celebratory ice cream is unlikely to set him off the rails anytime soon.

Being a world champion was not about to change

the boy from Devon. Indeed, even when an inevitable new flurry of media interest erupted afresh around him following his world title, Tom still came across as the same boy who had left for Rome. True, he was decorated with a world title now, but he remained as adorable as ever. In a chat with the *Daily Telegraph*, Tom explained how he was coming to terms with the issues fame throws up, including online impersonation. 'Someone is impersonating me on Twitter,' he said, with humorous annoyance. 'I'm *TomDaley1994* but everyone's suddenly started following *TomDaleyDiver*. I suspect it must be a girl because the tweets are really lame and un-cool and she puts kisses at the end – I'd hate anyone to think it was me.' Since those days he has become adept at using Twitter to communicate with his fans. He managed – after some time – to get his account 'verified' by Twitter, which means that everybody can see that his account is the genuine one. He also found a way to offer incentives to build his Twitter following.

Another development for Tom around this time was the preparation to move into his own bedroom at home. Having previously shared with his brother William, Tom was looking forward to the conversion of the family home's loft being completed so he could move into his own room up there. This was the life of Tom Daley as a fifteen-year-old: winning a world title, being a world famous sportsman . . . and sharing a bedroom with his brother. Despite his heartthrob status, he remained single. Aside from a rarely discussed brief relationship when he was thirteen, Tom has never acknowledged any romance in his life. For a while, it looked as if this was about to change. During 2009 and 2010, there were rumours of a flirtation between Tom and diver Pauline Ducruet, the daughter of Princess Stephanie of Monaco. The pair chatted via Facebook, and Tom claimed to his father that Ducruet was interested in him.

However, according to Rob, Tom did not want to take things further. 'I tried speaking to Tom about it as I was taking him to training but he didn't really want to make much of it,' he said. 'I don't know who introduced who to who, but she definitely has got a crush on him. Tom said to me, "She fancies me". I don't know what she said to him, though.' Ducruet certainly fits the mould of some other famous women Tom has spoken admiringly of. Others include Cheryl Cole and also the sister of the Duchess of Cambridge, Pippa Middleton. Their 'looks' are similar, suggesting there could be a theme developing. Either way, Tom seems thus far to prefer not to take advantage of the growing appeal he has to the fairer sex.

•

Away from actual competition and the ongoing commitments of his celebrity status, Tom had plenty else going on in 2009, a very busy year for him on a number of fronts. In July, Tom took part in 'Three Years to the Games', a ceremony to build excitement about the London 2012 Olympics, which entailed a visit to the Olympic Stadium to observe the continuing construction work. Wearing a hard hat and protective goggles alongside a similarly attired Lord Seb Coe, Tom enjoyed his visit: no one was more excited than him about the prospect of 2012. Here he continued to become the poster boy for the tournament, the young lad on whom the nation would pin its greatest hopes. Month by month his stature in this regard rose steadily, as the excitement for the tournament built up.

At the end of 2009, the year would become defined by one more thing, when Tom won the BBC's Young Sports Personality of the Year award once more. The ceremony was held on 13 December, and having reached the final shortlist, Tom faced opposition for the honour from tennis starlet Heather Watson and promising sprinter Jodie Williams. The judging panel was chaired by BBC Sport presenter John Inverdale and also included fellow presenter Jake Humphrey, *Blue Peter*'s Helen Skelton, *Sportsround* presenter Ore Oduba, previous Young Sports Personality of the Year winners swimmer Kate Haywood and sprinter Harry

Aikines-Aryeetey, and representatives of the Youth Sport Trust.

When it came to the big moment, it was Tom's name that was read out as the winner. He looked thrilled as he walked to the stage, dressed smartly in a sharp suit. 'Wow, thank you very much for this, it really does mean a lot,' he said as he was handed the award. He then thanked, 'all the people who have helped me this year', listing his parents, grandparents and coach, as well as Plymouth College. 'It's been a good year for me, and I'd just like to thank everybody who's helped me, so thank you very much,' he added. Among the other awards that Tom saw handed out that night were the Coach of the Year gong, which went to England football manager Fabio Capello, the Lifetime Achievement Award which was awarded to golf legend Seve Ballesteros, and the Sports Personality of the Year award itself, won by Manchester United footballer Ryan Giggs. (In addition to actually landing the 'Young Sports Personality' prize, Tom had also been nominated for the main one.)

It had been a particularly special honour for Tom, not least because this time he was there in person to receive it. 'An amazing night,' said the young diver looking back. 'I saw Jenson Button, Fabio Capello. Ryan Giggs was sat a couple of rows away. Cool.' His enthusiasm is touching, as is the fact that despite winning the award on the night, he was excited about seeing other sporting stars in the flesh, rather than crowing about his own accomplishment. Tom received some wise advice from boxer Amir Khan on the night. 'You should keep your family close to you, and the people you trust,' he told Tom. 'I kept my father close to me.'

After being named as Young Sports Personality of the Year Tom was told that he was the first person in history to win the award twice. 'I never knew that, and it really is such an honour to get this award,' he said. 'I still walk around here and see so many sporting legends and now they know who I am, that's the main thing!'

He was so excited to be there, even though it meant he would miss the final of his favourite television programme. 'BBC Sports Personality is definitely more important than *X Factor*, my friends are going to text me the result,' he said. Sure enough, a text came through confirming that Joe McElderry had won *The X Factor*. It was a good night for teenage boys *and* British television awards. A good month, indeed, for Tom had, just a few weeks earlier, also been named the *Plymouth Herald*'s Sports Personality of the Year. 'This year has been amazing and it's a real honour to get these two awards. It gives me a chance to recognize the support that Plymouth has given me,' he said. On the night he also was given the 'Champagne Moment of 2009' award for his historic victory in Rome, and was presented with his trophies by boxing legend Barry McGuigan.

•

The opening three events of 2010 were ones in which Tom learned, rather than won. In February, at the British Championships, he performed a new dive, the back two-and-a-half somersaults, two-and-a-half twists – also known as the 'twister' dive. However, his performance was not enough to win. Instead, he finished 40.05 points behind Peter Waterfield, who received three perfect 10s on what was a glorious day for him. Tom never recovered from having over-rotated on his armstand triple somersault dive.

After the event, coach Andy Banks hinted that there was an ongoing plan for Tom, from which the day's results would not deflect. Tom was also in philosophical mood, after his first outing since winning in Rome. 'Everyone has an off day but what pleased me was the new dive,' he said. He was not hiding his disappointment that he had not done better, but neither was he beating himself up about the result. 'I did make silly mistakes but then that's what happens in diving and hopefully I can correct them. I'm sure I am never going to make them again because I don't like feeling like this,' he said in an interview with the BBC.

He also had nothing but praise for Peter Waterfield, describing him as 'an incredible diver'. This was the first national competition Tom had failed at for four years, and he used this fact as added motivation. 'I'm going to go home and work my socks off,' he vowed.

'It's given me the kick up the backside I needed.'

In March, Tom flew to Qingdao in China for another competition. Again, the outcome was one of mixed feelings. On the positive side, Tom recorded his best score of the year in the 10-metre platform – 520.35. However, that was only enough to secure him a fourth-place finish. Qui Bo won in front of his home crowd.

April 2010 saw Tom fly to Mexico for the FINA Diving World Series event, which was held in Veracruz. In the men's 10-metre platform final he missed out on a podium place by the tightest of margins: just 0.8 points separating him and the home favourite, German Sánchez. Tom's 519.70 was his second-highest tally of the season so far. Then injury disrupted his progress. His tricep muscle played up and forced him to pull out of the European Championships in Budapest. 'It seems there may be a small tear,' said Tom of the damage to his tricep, caused while practising one of his new dives. 'The medical team and I felt it was best not to risk it and completely tear the muscle, which would put me out for three months and would see me miss the Commonwealth Games.'

The more immediate question was whether he should take part at the Youth Olympic Games in Singapore, just a week away. The decision was eventually taken that he should fly to Singapore and undergo a scan on his tricep once there, to determine whether or not he should compete. Tom was keen to take part, saying he would be 'gutted' if he did not. He was aware that just being in Singapore was of use to him as he prepared for the 2012 Olympics. 'It's all experience for London 2012, to be getting on the athlete buses and being in the athlete village,' he said.

Tom did compete, in the three-metre springboard diving competition, but his discomfort showed on the day and he finished far out of the podium places. He could only hope that by the time the Commonwealth Games came along, he would be recovered and on winning form.

In the meanwhile, however, in addition to all the extraordinary commitments in Tom's life, he also had all of the ordinary milestones to pass. These included educational ones – including his GCSE results. As all teenagers are when awaiting their results, Tom was nervous. The previous year, he had received A*s in Maths and English Language and an A in Science. This time he got two A*s – in Spanish and Photography – and an A in English Literature. He received the results by email, and clicked reply, sending a 'smiley face' in response.

'This year was all about my GCSEs, learning new dives and the Commonwealth Games,' he said as he celebrated his success. He chose to do A levels in Maths, Spanish and Photography.

•

As he was preparing for the Commonwealth Games, Tom was the subject of a BBC television documentary about his life. Made by the accomplished filmmaker Jane Treays, it was shot carefully over a long period of time, documenting the day-to-day life of Tom and his family. Sensing the potency of the father/son relationship between Tom and Rob, the programme-makers turned what might have been a standard profile of a young sporting talent into a touching portrayal of an eccentric, but ultimately heart-warming family relationship. Indeed, Rob became the unexpected star of the show, which portrayed him in all his slightly kooky glory. 'You don't get Tom Daley if you don't have Rob as who he is,' explained Tom's coach Andy Banks. Few would want it any other way.

Tom Daley: The Diver and His Dad was broadcast in October 2010, and from the start, it was a moving and unconventional affair. It opened with Tom lying on his bed at home in Plymouth, describing a terrible nightmare he had once endured about the London 2012 Olympics. In the nightmare, he was standing on the diving board at the Olympics, with just one more dive to get right in order to win the gold medal. 'And all of a sudden,' he said, 'I just see this shark come out from the bottom of the pool and just wait for me to land in it. And I'm thinking "Is that a shark there, or am I just thinking it?"'

In the dream, Tom dived and landed in the shark's mouth. 'I obviously died at the time, cos I got eaten by the shark.' The dream ended with him seeing news channels breaking the story of an Olympic diver dying because of a shark attack. 'That's very strange,' he conceded. 'I don't know what my imagination was doing then!'

There were plentiful scenes of ordinary family life in the Daley household. Debbie making Tom a meal, his brothers William and Ben playing games on the Wii. At one point, his brothers were asked what they thought of Tom's diving. After an awkward pause, William said 'It's pretty cool.' Ben then added, 'It's scary.' Asked if they were proud of Tom, both brothers replied with some reluctance in the positive. They were clearly finding the interview an uncomfortable experience, both of them a million miles away from Tom's polished media performances.

In one touching exchange they were asked if it was 'amazing to live with a world champion', to which Ben replied, 'No, *not* really.' William was horrified: 'Shut up!' he told his little brother. Ben replied: 'It's not!' Both boys have a healthy and balanced attitude towards their brother's fame. On the one hand, they are proud, on the other, they are aware that – for all his achievements and celebrity – Tom remains their big brother.

The scenes with Rob were particularly poignant. He spoke movingly of his battle with cancer, and his hopes for the future. 'I wonder if I'll make 2012, or see grandchildren,' he said. 'I think, why me?...But because I'm always laughing and joking, Tom thinks I'm fine.' His commitment and devotion to Tom was there for all to see. He showed the programme-makers the room where he hung all of Tom's medals, explaining how he had painstakingly measured the distance between the pins from which each medal was hung, in order to ensure that if the window was open the medals did not hit each other, creating the unwanted sound of a wind chime when he was trying to get to sleep.

Touching too were the scenes in which Tom and Rob interacted with one another. They made for quite a double-act. When Rob was shown collecting Tom from school, on the way home in the car, Rob asked his son why he was yawning. With a cheeky grin and a deliberately condescending tone, Tom replied, 'Yes, we'll go through this again: why, do people yawn?' Rob replied, 'Because they're tired, and why are you tired?' Tom replied: 'Because I'm tired!'

Later, they also crossed verbal swords about the route of the plane journey to Delhi. Tom stood his ground firmly, and after he left the room the journalist's voice was heard off-camera observing how competitive Tom is. Later, when his brother Ben showed he had won a certificate as 'fastest tie tier' in his class, Tom insisted he had previously won the same school prize. Both his parents contested Tom's claim in a good-humoured way.

Naturally, the 'infamous' press conference after the competition in Rome was mentioned in the documentary, central as it is to the narrative of Tom's relationship with his father. Andy Banks, who witnessed it at close hand, gave his thoughts on Rob's intervention. 'That was emotion spilling over,' said Banks. 'Rob has not got the degree in how to walk into a press centre and handle that moment.' Banks admitted there had been times since in which he wished he had held Rob back on the day. Overall, though, he backed up the feeling that there had been no harm done. Instead, the programme went on to show Rob as a devoted father, almost starstruck with awe by his own son. There was plenty of joshing between the two, including Tom pointing out the ticks and mannerisms Rob used that 'really annoy' him.

On Rob's illness, Tom remained rather tight-lipped. He spoke briefly of his plan to accompany Rob for a brain scan for the first time, calling it 'the scan for his brains and stuff'. His phrasing was awkward, almost certainly reflecting how uncomfortable Tom was discussing his father's illness. He tended to be unhappy discussing it in public, and journalists interviewing

Tom were warned in advance by his management that Rob's illness is off-limits during the interview.

It was the one topic for this otherwise publicity-comfortable young man that was basically a no-go area. But then what teenage boy would not feel upset about his sick father? He managed to smile about the hospital visit back at the house, saying he wanted to ask where the tumour was as they looked at the scans. Grinning, he said he had noticed his grandmother getting upset so chose not to. 'You kind of have to be brave to cope with it all,' he said of his father. In a separate scene, Rob could not recall what he had bought for Tom's sixteenth birthday, which was the following day. Given his devotion to his son, it was hauntingly clear that his illness was responsible for his memory lapse.

Tom's halo only slipped slightly – and momentarily – when he was shown as not in the best of moods in the morning, fobbing off his father's offer to cook breakfast for him. Rob called him 'Mr Grumpy', and Tom replied, 'No, Mr Just Woken Up'.

The documentary ended on a slightly unsatisfying note. Rob was still undergoing chemotherapy; Tom was yet to get to the Commonwealth Games, let alone London 2012. As a narrative climax, it was not a gold-medal-winning affair. At the end, with Tom overseas again and away from his father, he admitted he was missing Rob – and even his tendency to 'constantly wind me up'.

On broadcast, coinciding as it did with Tom's triumphant visit to the Commonwealth Games in Delhi, the programme really caught the public's imagination. In the *Daily Telegraph*, Chris Harvey reviewed the show, describing it as 'a warm, insightful glimpse of the prodigy at home and in the pool'. *Metro* newspaper's Keith Watson was also warmed by the show: 'It gave us a touching portrait of a father-and-son relationship that has somehow steered clear of the pitfalls of sporting obsession. They teased, they joshed, but their devotion was clear.' Even the *Guardian*'s notorious Sam Wollaston, a reviewer with a trademark for biting prose, was impressed with the subject of the programme. 'Tom seems lovely, a bit grumpy in the mornings as most sixteen-year-olds are, but otherwise a very likeable young man – polite, hard-working, dedicated, grounded,' he wrote. He was less impressed with the quality of the documentary itself, saying, 'It all falls a bit flat to be honest.'

Amol Rajan of *The Independent* was impressed with the programme: 'I don't think I've ever seen a father's love for his son presented more charmingly on the small screen.' However, he felt that the overall effect of the programme was unfair on Rob, and hinted at subtle ploys on the part of the programme-makers to this effect. 'What could not be made explicit, but was very obvious, was the contrast between father and son.

The former's unrefined West Country accent rubbed up against young Tom's slightly effete manner. Fat, balding, tumour-ridden Dad wore lifeless surfing T-shirts; muscular, naked Tom was blossoming into manhood.'

This seemed a strange issue to read so much into as there are few men in their forties who would look impressive next to a sixteen-year-old athlete. However, at least *The Times* was kinder to Rob, while praising Tom. 'Yet Tom emerged as a sixteen-year-old blessed not only with talent and good looks but the nicest temperament you could imagine,' wrote Andrew Billen, adding, 'The same applied to his besotted, dedicated father.'

•

While the nation was absorbed in the TV series, Tom was en route to Delhi for the 2010 Commonwealth Games. He had looked forward to them immensely, but a series of controversies threatened to derail not just his involvement, but the entire event. The run-up to the tournament saw a slew of horror stories surrounding the organization of the event, including sensational headlines about the threat of a monsoon-flood, swimmers falling ill after training in the official pools, concerns that the stadiums would not be completed in time, fears of a terror attack and then a freak car accident involving Ugandan officials. It became the most colourful and worrying build up to a Commonwealth Games tournament that anyone could remember.

Once the games did get underway, the security measures undertaken by the organizers seemed draconian and drew a surprised reaction. Spectators had coins, keys and sunscreen taken from them on arrival at venues, one even had his paperback book confiscated. The authorities were obviously not taking any chances. Tom could only try and focus on his preparation, rather than these negative stories. He would join athletes from seventy-one nations who would between them compete in seventeen different sports over the eleven-day tournament.

He had suffered from a tricep injury in the run-up to the games, and he knew he would have to 'do something special' to succeed. And he did just that. In the 10-metre platform competition, he completed what was described as 'a perfect dive'. Going into the final round, there were just two points between him and the Olympic champion Matthew Mitcham, so things could hardly have been more tense. Tom had finished second in the qualifiers, which meant he went first in the final round.

Later, he said that the moment he hit the water he knew it had been a good dive. Only when he emerged again from the water did he see the 10s across the board. He knew then that Mitcham would need to average nine points from the judges with his final dive. 'That was a very happy moment for me,' said Tom.

His fellow British athletes were impressed. 'He pulled it out of the bag when he needed to,' said an admiring Max Brick, who had watched, cheering, from the sidelines.

'I got my entries okay,' added Tom with modest understatement. Rob had not flown to Delhi, but he managed to pull off a kind of reprise of the 'press conference incident' during an interview on Radio Five Live, when Tom was linked direct back to his father at home in Devon. Asked if he had a message for his son, Rob said, 'Erm, well, I suppose I could sing him a song?' Tom was immediately embarrassed, 'Oh no – you can't sing me a song,' he said. 'We're live on radio!' Naturally, the presenters encouraged Rob to sing and he did so, with a few lines of ' Oleh . . . oleh, oleh, oleh', followed by a cheeky chuckle. Listeners could only imagine Tom's embarrassment.

Then came the synchro dive, which Tom was to perform alongside his partner Max Brick. There was plenty of reason for caution. Since the World Championships in Rome in 2009, Tom had only been able to complete twenty days of synchro training with his partner. Moreover, the field was extremely strong, particularly the Australian contingent, including Matthew Mitcham.

'It was a very tough event but we have been putting a lot of work in,' Tom told BBC Five Live. 'We did one of the hardest dives in our list but we pulled it off today and we got a massive personal best as well. We wanted to come here and do well and to get the gold was the icing on the cake.'

It was Brick's first major medal. Again, Tom was asked about how comfortable he felt with the media attention. 'Yes, I do enjoy the media stuff,' he told the BBC. 'It's something that I'd like to do when I've finished diving, something that I'd like to go into.'

By now, Tom had indeed become an accomplished and polished interviewee, though he was also developing a tendency to begin nearly every answer: 'Yeah, definitely.' This was a small chink in an otherwise impressive, eloquent armour.

CHAPTER TEN

•

Team Daley

'Would I date a fan?'
TOM DALEY

THE AUTHOR WAS PRESENT WHEN TOM arrived back in Britain from the Commonwealth Games in October 2010. The 'arrivals' areas of airport terminals are normally places of mixed emotions. Chauffeurs stand rigidly, holding cards bearing the name of the passengers they are due to whisk off in their cars. Passengers sleep fitfully on benches, awoken by businessmen speaking loudly into their mobile phones. Meanwhile, families stand, full of excitement, waiting to welcome home their loved ones from foreign shores.

The emotional embraces that take place when families are reunited is always heart-warming and was immortalized in the feel-good film *Love, Actually*. Thanks to films like that, airports have become overly romanticized places, the reality often less exciting than the dream. As we awaited the return of Tom's flight from Delhi, I spoke with a few press photographers. Two of them had 'airside passes' so they had already spoken to Tom as he waited at the luggage carousel. These were tough tabloid snappers, who down the years have been evaded and roughed-up by countless celebrities. When I asked them how they found Tom to deal with, their hardened faces softened into smiles. 'Oh, he is *very* nice,' they said. They said there was a rumour that Tom's father was planning a bit of drama. I also spoke with Tom's father Rob, who was naturally excited to see his son. He said he planned to run to Tom and give him a big soppy hug. Sadly, he did not follow through with this and we were not to witness first hand another moment of cute, paternally delivered embarrassment for Tom.

Then Tom appeared, not looking in any way like someone who had just endured a ten-hour flight. Instead he looked fresh as ever. I asked him how it felt to win gold out in Delhi. 'It felt great,' he said, 'I definitely didn't expect it.'

He then embraced his father and began posing for photographs. He didn't need to be asked twice to produce his medals for a photograph. When some fans appeared asking for snaps with him he obliged every time. He didn't seem to be 'tolerating' this attention, he seemed to be enjoying it. As more and more people gathered round, Tom had his photograph taken with passengers from round the world. It was like a United Nations of fans. He had announced the details of his flight's arrival on his Facebook page before setting off from India. Perhaps he had hoped for a crowd of fans to come to the airport especially to see him.

It would have been hard for many of his teenage fan-base to drop everything and travel straight to Heathrow on this autumn night. True, if it had been a pop idol there might have been a screaming mob. The same would go for a football team returning having won a trophy. For Tom, he might find that his appeal and the intensity of his admirers will increase in years to come. Particularly if he manages to make the transition from sport to full-time television work.

For good examples of this transition he can look to many people. Devonian Sue Barker was a tennis star for many years, reaching the semi-finals of Wimbledon and winning the French Open, on her way to becoming number three in the world. She has since become a well-known and loved sports presenter on the BBC, satellite television and in Australia as well. Other sportsmen and women who have built successful television careers include Gary Lineker, Clare Balding, Steve Cram, Ian Wright and Matthew Pinsent. These people have worked almost exclusively in sports broadcasting, but Tom's television ambitions go beyond that.

Tom's oft-repeated specific ambition is to be a *Blue Peter* presenter. He already has a connection with the show, having won a gold badge from Blue Peter in 2009 in recognition of the inspiration he had given to young people throughout the year. Formula One champion Jenson Button, sprinter Usain Bolt, heptathlon champion Jessica Ennis and Take That front-man Gary Barlow were among the other figures thus honoured that year. Others on the list included the England women's cricket team, Comic Relief broadcaster Lenny Henry and *Horrid Henry* author Francesca Simon.

'We know that their achievements will inspire our young viewers to aim high as they grow up,' said *Blue Peter* editor Tim Levell. The *Blue Peter* team visited Devon to present Tom with his badge. Writing about the experience on the SportsVibe website, Tom put the honour in its context: 'The BBC's *Blue Peter* team also came down to my home in Plymouth to present me with a coveted gold badge and that, believe me, is up there with the World Championships diving gold medal.'

As 2010 came to a close, further confirmation of Tom's stature was provided when he won the BBC Young Sports Personality of the Year award for an unprecedented third time. He looked more relaxed as he walked to the stage to collect the award, having been patted on the back in celebration by Rob who was sitting next to him in the arena. 'This comes very unexpected, I've got so many people to thank it's unbelievable,' he said as he accepted the award. 'I'd like to thank my family, grandparents, Max Brick my diving partner, and my strength and conditioning coaches. It's been a tough year for me with injury but to go to the Commonwealth Games as my main event of the year, I was very happy to come away with two gold medals so thank you very much.'

Again, he had also been up for the main award, this time it went to A.P. McCoy, the Northern Irish racehorse jockey.

The other highlight for Tom and his family in the closing months of 2010 was a trip to Disneyland Paris. It was a lovely day for the family, who joshed and teased each other with fondness. Rob sat out the rides that the other family members daringly went on, sensibly holding their coats as they sought out ever more scary thrills. For Tom, this meant his love of adrenaline rushes could be satisfied during some rare downtime from his training commitments. Ever-present behind their fun was the hope that Rob would pull through his ongoing battle against cancer, meaning that many more joyful days out could occur.

•

Tom is cleverly building his fan-base and connecting with it online. His official website (TomDaley.TV) is the main portal for his online presence, and he was involved in the design of it, insisting on certain features and themes. 'I've made sure my website is video-based so it reaches out to more of my age group,' he said. He also uses Twitter. On 16 January 2011, Tom treated his Twitter followers to his first 'Twitcam' session. He appeared nervous during it and admitted that he didn't really know what to do or say. For the first sixty seconds he seemed unaware he was on camera and broadcasting. 'Right,' he said when he was ready to start. 'I'm only on for five or so minutes.' He then sat looking unsure of what to say, before asking, 'Anything good on TV at the moment?' Finally, he began to get more into the spirit of it and responded to calls for 'shout-outs' to the fans watching.

He suggested fans could ask him questions, but the quality of the subsequent discussion was not high-adrenalinee stuff. Asked what music he liked he said, 'Stuff like the Black Eyed Peas, or whatever is in the charts.' There was just time for him to say that one of his favourite treats was ice cream before he called an end to the Twitcam. The most entertaining part of the session had been when his brothers had an argument within earshot of the camera, prompting Tom to ask them to shut up, because 'they can hear'. He then spoke briefly about some synchro-training he had been doing in Leeds the previous week alongside Peter Waterfield, and how excited he was for the nationals in Southend. Someone asked him what the difference is between 'Twitcam' and 'BlogTV'. Tom shrugged his shoulders and looked puzzled.

He returned later the same day for a second Twitcam. During this he answered questions from the fans. Asked if he had ever had a diving accident, he confirmed that he had hit his head on the board on two occasions. 'Quite scary, but nothing to stop me from diving,' he said. 'And, yes, I have done a belly flop before,' he added. He said that his 'dream celeb' is Cheryl Cole. During pauses between such questions-and-answers he plugged his official website and official Facebook page. Asked what his favourite colour is, he replied, 'I would be boring and say blue – blue is pretty much my favourite colour.'

For his next Twitcam session, some weeks later, Tom had put more thought and preparation into it, guaranteeing a more insightful experience for all. Via his Twitter page, he invited his followers to send him questions ahead of the session. From those submitted, he chose twenty questions and made answering them the mainstay of the session. Before he could get going on the questions, though, he was interrupted by a phone-call from his auntie. It was a moment that added extra authenticity and charm to proceedings.

One fan asked if he ever felt self-conscious wearing just his Speedos in front of people when he dived. 'No you don't, actually,' he explained, 'because everybody is wearing them and it is something that is easy to move around in. I guess I just kind of got used to it from an early age.' In response to the fan who asked if he would ever date a fan he perked up. 'Good one,' he said with a twinkle in his eyes. 'You never know, I guess they would understand about the diving. So . . . who knows, who knows?' However, the only female he seemed in any hurry to get together with was Cheryl Cole. He inserted her into three of his answers, including asking who in the world, alive or dead, he would most like to spend a day with.

Tom has always made it clear that whoever he goes out with will have to be respectful of his diving ambitions, which are little less than an obsession in his life. His competitive streak is unlikely to loosen its grip long enough on him to allow him to be distracted.

Rob was once asked during an interview if he expected Tom to capitalize on his fame and good looks by taking up with a pop star girlfriend, buying a mansion together and being interviewed for *Hello!* magazine. 'I don't think he'd be impressed by that,' said Rob. 'It's hard to say because he hasn't even had a proper girlfriend yet. There just isn't the time with all his training, and I can honestly say that when it does happen, she will have to be prepared to come second to the diving.'

Back at the Twitcam session, Tom also said he loved photography because, 'it is something that is quite relaxing', and admitted that he had no idea what he would be doing had he not made it as a diver, beyond hoping it would have been another sport. He was asked which famous singers he would choose to form a boyband with. He chose Justin Bieber, Justin Timberlake, Taio Cruz and Usher. He spoke fondly of Italy, saying, 'I love Rome, I love the ice cream there and the Italian food' but said that his favourite place was Texas. He spoke three times of his dream of becoming a television presenter and plugged his website again. It was all more focused and professional than before, but even the unpolished moments brought their own charm.

His next Twitcam session was in April, as he relaxed at home midway through the World Series events. Once more, he had trailed the session on his Twitter account, guaranteeing plentiful interest from his devoted fans online. Again, he asked for questions to be sent ahead of the chat, and gave a teasing hint that some strange ones were being sent when he tweeted: 'Keep them coming . . . some of them are pretty interesting haha :/' a few days ahead of the arrangement.

Held on an unseasonably sunny April Sunday morning, he had timed the session in part to work for his many fans in the Far East, particularly the Chinese. He began the session speaking about his recent experiences in Beijing, where he had bagged a bronze medal. Then, he turned to the questions, including: if diving didn't exist, what would you be doing now? 'I have no idea what I'd be doing right now, I'd probably still be at school. I'd like to get into media. I quite like Spanish and I quite like photography, so there's a few things I could be doing.'

He also spoke of his love of Easter and said that the celebrity he would most want to dive with would be Cheryl Cole – (yet again!). He said his favourite film would be one out of *Avatar*, *Flushed Away* or *Inception*. 'Anything funny, really, and anything interesting, I guess.' He was asked if his trunks had ever fallen down as he hit the water from a dive. 'Yes,' he said with slight embarrassment, 'plenty of times.' Added Tom: 'I've actually hit the water and my trunks have gone right down to my ankles, which is quite amusing. You have to pull them up quite quickly, before you get to the surface.'

A more insightful question was asked about how he coped with the experience of appearing on a stage in front of a large audience, or on television in front of millions of viewers. 'I guess you are under pressure, you just have to cope with it.' Another, *Smash Hits* style question, was: what is the most important thing you own? 'Obviously, medals are quite important,' he said. 'But, I'd say my phone is the thing I always need and the thing I always have to have on me.'.

Asked who he would be for a day he said: 'I would be Simon Cowell . . . someone with a lot of power.'

Another questioner wondered what Tom did about nerves ahead of and during diving events. 'There's not much you can do to calm your nerves, you just need to focus on what you need to do and how all the training's been going and that sort of stuff. If you start thinking too much about it, you get even more nervous.'

Among the other revelations from Tom during the session were:

'I can't play any instruments or sing. I used to sing – but not any more. It's been diving for a long time now, so that's kind of what I do now.'

'The place I would most like to visit is St Lucia, because I can remember doing a school project on it.'

'I'd like to sky-dive rather than swim with sharks if I had to choose, as I've already swam with sharks.'

He also broke the news that the goldfish he had been given for his sixteenth birthday, which had featured in the BBC documentary, had sadly passed away. Later, in a chat with the *Guardian*, Tom expanded on the run of poor fortune he has had with pet goldfish. 'Every time

I go away my parents forget to feed it or overfeed it, or something like that. Apparently my last one, one of its fins stopped working and it was swimming round in a circle. I've had bad luck with goldfish.'

Looking ahead to the World Series, Tom tried to mobilize his fans to attend his meetings. 'Hopefully there will be a big Tom Daley contingent there to give me support,' he said. He even directed them on how much noise they were allowed to make during diving events. 'When [the diver is] on the board, you can cheer as loud as you can,' he said. 'But as soon as the whistle blows, then you have to be quiet until the person's hit the water.'

He had honed his 'Twitcam' technique well, and this seemed an ideal way for Tom to keep building his fan-base and to keep them interested in him going forward.

His profile in the mainstream media continued to soar during 2010, including a place on the panel of the Sky television sporting panel show *A League of Their Own*, and an appearance as a 'mystery guest' on the BBC's *A Question of Sport*. The panel guessed it was Tom thanks to, as captain Phil Tufnell put it, 'those lovely little big brown eyes'.

•

Meanwhile, bad news was on the cards for Tom and his family. At the end of January 2011, Rob was diagnosed as having a second brain tumour. Worryingly, he was told the growth was 'aggressive', which was devastating news for Rob and his family, who had hoped to have seen the end of the illness. Having been plagued by increasingly painful headaches, Rob had visited the doctor for a check-up. After making the usual checks and scans, the doctors gave Rob the bad news. Things were getting worse. 'I woke up in the middle of the Saturday night with excruciating headaches,' Rob recalled in the *Plymouth Herald*. 'Debbie got me paracetamol. That didn't work. Then she got my ibuprofen, but that didn't help.'

Naturally, they feared the worst. 'She rang the emergency number I have and asked what else she could give me,' continued Rob. He was hurriedly taken to Derriford Hospital, in Crownhill, Plymouth. When the doctors discovered that it was the tumour causing this pain, they gave Rob steroids to reduce the swelling. 'We didn't really think it was related to the new tumour, which was obviously naive on our part. We thought it was just a bad headache at first. It meant I lost mobility on my left side. As the swelling went down, I could finally start to work on getting my mobility back, but it was a long struggle.'

During those testing times, the father once more

looked to his son for inspiration. 'While I was in hospital I was constantly trying to move my arm and legs so I did not lose my range of movement more than I already had,' Rob said. 'Always in the back of my mind was, "I have been walking for forty years – why can't I do it now? If Tom can do what he does – learn a front four-and-a-half – I can get on my feet."'

While outsiders looked at Rob and marvelled at his courage, Rob was always so busy marvelling at Tom that he did not see how great he himself was. 'He knows he has to do the [front four-and-a-half] dive to win an Olympic medal because the Russians, the Chinese, even the Cubans are doing it,' said Rob of Tom. 'It is so hard, it wasn't easy for him to accept he had to learn it. It took him month after month. I said I just have to keep going, too.'

As for Tom, he was heroic as well, by all accounts. He visited his father in hospital and did his best to keep Rob's spirits up. He often marvelled at how Rob had kept his surreal sense of humour, even during the painful and fearful times. Tom pushed Rob's wheelchair whenever he was needed. Naturally, the experience was one that the family found humour in. 'All the boys and Debbie joked that we were Lou and Andy from *Little Britain*,' Rob told the *Plymouth Herald*.

Humour could not dispel the fact that this certainly was a terrifying time for the whole family, not least

Rob. However, he made sure he praised the medical team at the Derriford Hospital. 'I want to thank all the oncology staff and all the staff in Brent Ward,' he said. 'They are giving me two hundred per cent care. It is second-to-none care and they are constantly monitoring me. It's incredible.' There was no disguising the scale of the challenge he faced, as he was clear to express. 'It's horrible and the treatment is a lot stronger,' he said. 'I am on a lot more steroids to reduce the swelling. But I am in the best place for where I need to be now.'

When Rob got home, he went through the gruelling process of trying to return to normal fitness levels. His mind had been restless and he was ready for the challenge. 'As soon as my condition was stable and I was able to move around again, I went up [the stairs] on my backside and pulled myself up using the balustrades,' he said. 'I was determined to get up there. I can walk up there now. If I need help, I have people around me.'

As for Tom, he made little public comment about his father's illness. His only statement was sent to his followers via Twitter, after he had visited his father in hospital. 'My dad never seems to lose his sense of humour,' he wrote.

It was left to Tom's management company to make a more detailed announcement. 'The last scan results Rob received on 28 January showed that he had a second tumour,' said a spokeswoman. 'This meant the chemotherapy treatment had to change and doctors have been running a series of tests and scans, in hospital, to monitor the situation.'

Rob spoke to the *Plymouth Herald* about his new setback, the challenge it raised, and how Tom was once more helping him to get through these testing times. 'I know that one day I will be up and out again, and I will look back at this stage of my life and see it as a temporary setback,' said Rob. 'I have to be up and about soon because we have a small competition coming up next year. Seeing Tom compete at the Olympics is my aim and focus, and there is no way I am missing that. Tom is fully understanding of my situation and he knows what is going on. I think it drives him and gives him even more focus to achieve. Knowing him he wants to work hard.'

It was touching to hear how father and son both derived so much strength from one another at such a difficult time. Of course, Rob's illness was a challenge for the whole family and also for Rob's friends. He was such a likeable man that it was difficult for any who knew him not to feel a real sense of injustice over what he was facing. When he had first been diagnosed with cancer, Rob could not help but ask: 'Why me?' Those who knew and loved him felt similarly, including, of course, Tom.

To help him cope with the strain of watching his

father battle cancer, Tom had taken comfort and inspiration from the example of cycling legend Lance Armstrong. Tom has said he admires Armstrong 'because of all the stuff he's been through'. All the 'stuff' Armstrong has been through includes a heroic, against-all-odds battle with cancer. On 2 October 1996, Armstrong was diagnosed with stage three testicular cancer. So advanced was the cancer that it had spread to his lungs, abdomen and brain. He was told that his chance of survival was under forty per cent. One doctor told him to go home and get his affairs in order as quickly as he could, because he was going to die and there was nothing that could be done to stop this.

Instead, however, Armstrong miraculously beat the cancer and was back in training for cycling just fifteen months later. What happened next was beyond a miracle: in 1999 he won the sport's biggest event, the Tour de France, and then broke cycling records by winning it seven consecutive times.

He has become a sporting icon, but is also so much more. Armstrong is an inspiration to the cancer community across the world. Prior to his illness he had competed in the Tour de France, but never won it. The fact he defeated advanced cancer and then broke all Tour de France records has brought encouragement and comfort to many who have been troubled and tested by the disease.

The Livestrong charity he founded to help fight cancer has become a vibrant movement, and is also iconic, thanks to the yellow wristbands worn by its supporters – the first 'charity wristbands' to exist. Over 70 million yellow Livestrong wristbands have been sold. It's no wonder Tom is so inspired by Armstrong's twin narratives: the defeat of cancer, and sporting success. The former cyclist constitutes a remarkable example to all, including Tom who said he was 'inspired' when he read Armstrong's remarkable, best-selling memoir, *It's Not About the Bike*. Tom also follows the cyclist's popular Twitter account.

In the meantime, Rob tried his utmost to make day-to-day life as normal as possible. 'I still shine the boys' shoes on a Sunday night, ready for the morning, and come Sunday I'll be doing that as normal,' he said. 'That might sound old-fashioned to some, but so be it. It's what dads do, in my book. Mine did it for me, and my boys will hopefully do it for their kids, when they have them. I just have to make sure I hang around long enough to see that.' Asked if he would be able to watch Tom take part in London 2012 if his illness persisted, Rob was unequivocal: 'Even if I have to go on my hands and knees, I'll be there.'

CHAPTER ELEVEN

•

Mind Games

'I don't want to get carried away but in the synchro, I
think I'm right in saying that's the first time the Chinese
have been beaten in a World Series final.'
ANDY BANKS, diving coach

Tom's next challenge in the winter of 2010/2011 was
in the National Cup at Southend. Paired with Olympic
silver medallist Peter Waterfield, they finished the
first day with a gold medal, after finishing on top of
the tree in the synchro competition. The next day Tom
was tantalizingly close to another gold, this time in
the 10-metre platform. During a nail-biting final, both
Daley and Waterfield held the lead at different times,
as among their dives they performed the front four-
and-a-half somersaults tucked.

Tom was in the lead at the halfway point, but it
was Waterfield who finished with gold. Tom took
silver, and looked on the bright side as best as his

competitive, winning mentality would allow him to. 'It is obviously disappointing to not win the title, but I had a really long year last year and I just need to take the positives from this performance and come back stronger in my next competition,' he told the *Plymouth Herald*. He had totalled 472 points, which was short of the winner Waterfield (494) but comfortably ahead of guest diver from Sweden, Christofer Eskilsson, who scored 414 points, and fellow Brit Max Brick (399).

Tom also won silver in the men's three-metre springboard competition, one that he is not a regular in by any means. Nevertheless, he gained 419 points, which left him just a whisker behind Brazilian guest competitor Cesar Castro, with 428 points, and reasonably close to the winner Jack Laugher, who was on 458 points. Looking at his gold-winning performance with Waterfield on day one, Tom was full of beans. And rightly so, as he and Waterfield had outclassed City of Leeds pair Joe Meszaros and Callum Johnstone, and the third-placed pairing of James Denny and Max Brick. 'The first two dives were a very high standard,' he said. 'That was probably the best we've ever done them, which is really encouraging.' The sell-out Southend crowd, and indeed everyone in Britain who was looking ahead to London 2012, felt encouraged too. The Daley–Waterfield axis was in good health.

In Russia in March, both Tom and Tonia Couch struggled when they competed in the FINA series. Tom finished fifth in the men's individual 10-metre platform competition final at the World Series tournament with a total of 459 points. The winner, China's Qiu Bo, was a long away ahead of that with 607 points. Meanwhile, Couch and her diving partner Rebecca Gallantree could only finish sixth in the final of the 10-metre platform.

Tom's performance was in a sense more respectable than the position suggested, because he had been expecting to dive in partnership with Peter Waterfield. However, Waterfield fell ill just days before the tournament, meaning Tom had less than forty-eight hours notice that he would be competing individually. This was a blow from the selectors at Team GB's point of view, who remained keen for the pair to continue working on forging a strong partnership. 'The first leg of the World Series is important as it sets the tone for the rest of the competition,' Tom explained. 'It's the first time this year a lot of divers have competed against each other, so I suppose you get a taste of what's to come in 2011!'

Andy Banks put the result into a reasonable context. 'To be fair to Tom, Pete picking up a virus and being confined to bed for two days meant he was suddenly in an individual competition against some of the best operators in the world,' he told the This Is Plymouth website. 'He didn't get the entry right in his new four-and-a-half front tuck dive and that affected his total. But, they're in China this weekend, so we'll see how it goes there, but it's all about getting things right now that matters.'

Then it was on to Beijing for the second World Series competition, where Tom dived alongside a recovered Peter Waterfield in the 10-metre synchro. They won bronze, after the gold was seized by Cao Yuan and Zhang Yanquan of China. Separating the English and Chinese divers were a pair of Germans, Sascha Klein and Patrick Hausding.

As before, Andy Banks was on hand with some positive and supportive reflections on Tom's performance. He told BBC Sport: 'Them training together now is paying off and we're very pleased with the result. It was a very good performance by them both and they look so natural in the synchro. It's still early days, so watch this space with them really – but they're certainly the "A" team for London 2012. I think it's a very exciting prospect for London. Given that the Germans are right up there, to be so close to them on their first hit is great. Myself and Lindsey Fraser, Pete's coach, are both very pleased with it.'

In the individual dives twenty-four hours later,

Tom was eclipsed by Waterfield. Tom failed to reach the final of the 10-metre platform competition after finishing fifth, while Waterfield grabbed a bronze. It was another reminder for the public that, for all the hype that surrounds Tom, it is his partner who is the more accomplished athlete. 'Tom will be disappointed at not making the individual final, but it's all down to inconsistency with his new tariff of dives,' said Banks, ever the optimist. 'He can deliver them no problem in training, but it's frustrating that he isn't able to all of the time during competition. And, at this level against the world's best divers, you cannot afford not to.'

He then put the two days in context, and looked at the bigger picture. 'But the big result as far as I'm concerned is that Tom and Peter have proved they can compete at the top level as synchro partners,' he said. 'There's no doubt they are Team GB's number one duo, but they hadn't had chance to show what they could do against world-class divers. But on their [international] debut in Beijing, they really worked well together, which bodes well for the future. The good thing about the pairing is that there is a healthy competition going on there. Tom knows that if he lets his standards drop, Pete won't need a second invitation to take advantage. And likewise, Pete is acutely aware, as we all are, of Tom's talent and competitiveness.

If Pete is not at the top of his game, then Tom will quickly sense it and make him pay. So, this scenario, hopefully, is a win-win situation for Great Britain and for Tom's development.' Still to come were the next two legs of the series, which would take place in Sheffield and then Mexico.

There was increased public interest in Tom's partnership with Waterfield, and therefore in Waterfield himself. Who was this lesser-known, more senior young man who dived alongside the nation's poster boy? *The Independent on Sunday* described Waterfield as 'wallowing in the shadow of Tiny Tom'. The article complained that the attention afforded the 'teen sensation' overshadowed the fact that Waterfield was the more decorated diver, who had, of course, just beaten Tom in Beijing. 'To be honest, I've always expected to beat him,' Waterfield told the newspaper. 'When I was out with my injury [he needed shoulder surgery in 2008], everyone seemed to write me off, and it was during this time that Tom really came through. I had a point to prove to myself more than anything, I wanted to show that I am still the best in Britain.'

He agreed that Tom's level of fame and popularity dwarfed his own, but while admitting he would not object to a little more attention himself, he was careful to not sound resentful of Tom. 'He's like a little pop star,' said Waterfield. 'He's so good and such a nice lad, it's quite right he gets all this attention. It doesn't worry me at all because it not only helps him, it helps our sport. Sometimes I think it would be nice to get a bit of it myself but I don't really expect it so I'm not going to sit here and complain.'

Naturally, he was asked about Tom's partnership with Blake Aldridge. Waterfield dodged that thorny topic, choosing instead to paint a positive portrait of how he gets along with young Mr Daley. 'I don't really know the ins and outs of their relationship but what matters to me is that we get on brilliantly as partners as well as friends,' he said. 'He says he can learn a lot from me because of my experience but actually I can learn a lot from him. I don't feel at all like a big brother, more of a mate.'

Lest the article be viewed as an attempt to put a wedge between Waterfield and Tom, the latter was commissioned to provide his own input, in the form of a sidebar article entitled 'Message from an icon'. In it, he paid tribute to his partner and spoke of how they complemented one another. 'I have huge admiration for Pete and it's great that he has already got an Olympic silver medal,' Tom wrote. 'He's had first-hand experience of being on the podium and that's invaluable to me. He has said himself that we make a good team because he brings the experience and I bring the enthusiasm.'

He added that there was no issue with the fact that they would dive together as partners, and then dive competitively in the individual heats. As far as Tom was concerned, these complement rather than contradict one another. 'Obviously we both aspire to a place on the podium at London 2012, as individuals and as a pair,' he continued. 'When we need to work as a team, we work well and when we compete individually we act like rivals. Obviously then it's very competitive but there are definitely no hard feelings out of the pool. We get on really well.'

So the signs boded well for Sheffield and Mexico in the near future, and for London 2012 looking further ahead. For Tom, 2012 was always on his mind. While he was careful to focus on the immediate, it was difficult to keep a lid on his excitement. The synchro event remains Tom's brightest chance of a medal in London. 'It's early days, but it looks like the combination of Pete and Tom is going to work out,' Andy Banks told the *Plymouth Herald* ahead of the Sheffield meeting. 'They're both very competitive and each one knows if he lets his standards drop for a moment, then the other will take advantage. So, Tom has to make sure his dive tariff is right on the button every time, and in his defence, they are very difficult. But Tom can do all of them. It's only a matter of time before they're part of his programme – and then watch out.'

However, at this stage in his career, Tom was under pressure and this was being noted. Combining his diving commitments and challenges with his education (he was preparing for his A-levels), and also his interest in maintaining a wider public profile, kept him very busy. For a lad his age he was travelling a great deal around the world, itself a time-consuming and draining experience. With new dives to learn there was a lot on his plate. 'These new dives are very tough, but we'll get there, I've no doubts about that, or Tom's ability,' said Banks. But there was no disguising the challenges ahead, and it was vital at this stage that the situation was handled correctly to avoid burnout ahead of the Olympics on which Tom and his family had for so long pinned their hopes.

In May 2011 the Olympic torch began its journey around England, passing through Tom's home city of Plymouth. 'It will be great for the city of Plymouth to see it,' said Tom ahead of the day. As these developments were mounting for him, Tom had become the literal poster boy for the London Olympics, having for so long been the metaphorical one. Huge posters advertising tickets for the tournament were plastered across massive billboards nationwide, as well as in full-page slots in national newspapers, including *The Times*. These posters featured a trunks-clad Tom doing a handstand in front of a backdrop of the capital city and its Olympic stadium. If anyone was under any doubt that Tom was the lead hope for Britain for 2012, these posters were enormous reminders of this fact.

There seemed to be little soul-searching, publicly at least, over whether the increasing promotion of this young teen had an unhealthy angle to it. In football, when young players such as Michael Owen, Wayne Rooney or Theo Walcott were thrust into the public imagination as figures on which the national team's hopes could rest, many onlookers urged caution and reminded people of the tender years of the player in question. In some cases this worked well, with Michael Owen being protected from the extraordinary hype that exploded around him after his starring role against Argentina during the 1998 World Cup Finals. As a result, Owen went on to star again and again for the national team, including a memorable hat-trick in Germany in 2001. In contrast, Theo Walcott has never fully bounced back from the fuss that greeted his shock selection for the 2006 World Cup, as an inexperienced seventeen-year-old. For the long-term, we must hope that Daley follows in the path of Owen's career (though hopefully becoming a bigger success) rather than Walcott's.

As we have seen, the footballer Daley looks up to and admires is David Beckham. Just as Beckham became known as 'golden balls' so has Daley been dubbed 'the golden boy'. With Daley keen on building a wider career as a celebrity from a young age, he clearly has that ambition and focus that served Beckham so well. Daley's more humble nature will serve to put him on a different, but related path. Again, the timing is fortuitous. Tom has come into the public eye at a time when we have grown wary of those who chase fame too keenly. With difficult times financially placing extra strain on us all, we are no longer so keen on stars who ostentatiously chase and flaunt wealth. Instead the public want someone we believe is a little bit more 'like us' – and Tom is a perfect character to fill that brief. A boy from Devon could only ever carry a wholesome, grounded air. The south west of England is simply not associated with arrogance, greed or attention-seeking.

Tom's stature was re-confirmed when he took part in a comical sketch organized by actor James Corden for Comic Relief 2011. This was the second time that Corden had chosen Daley to be part of a Comic Relief sketch, after the pair had co-starred in a sketch the previous year. Among those who took part were Justin Bieber, Sir Paul McCartney and Ringo Starr, Keira Knightley, George Michael, Rio Ferdinand and former Prime Minister Gordon Brown. Also present in the huge, star-studded cast-list were boyband JLS, and television presenters Dermot O'Leary, Clare

Balding and Richard Madeley. Adding to the teenage appeal were *Harry Potter* stars Rupert Grint and Tom Felton. The sketch helped define Comic Relief's most successful fundraising year ever. By the time the broadcast closed at 2 a.m., an unprecedented £74 million had been raised.

•

So to Sheffield, where talk was of just how far the Daley/Waterfield partnership could ultimately go. Waterfield compared his partnership with Tom with that of his previous partner, Leon Taylor. 'Leon and I had been diving together for ten years, I think, before Athens, so this is a lot younger as a partnership,' he told the BBC. 'But Tom and I have come together and we've gelled really quickly – and we're only improving every time we train. Normally it'd take a while but because Tom is so talented we're working hard and working together well.'

As for Tom, he spoke positively of the partnership also. He again emphasized that he welcomed and relished the chance to dive alongside an Olympic medal-winning diver such as Waterfield. 'We're improving all the time, definitely,' he said. 'We can do well. Diving in front of a sell-out home crowd will be amazing.' Added Tom: 'We got a bronze medal at the last World Series [in Beijing] and that was a British record as well. There are a lot of people who could win it [in Sheffield]. There's the Chinese and then you've got the Russians and the Australians, Americans – there are so many potential winners out there.'

Tom added that he was not expecting to win an individual medal over the weekend, even though he was aware that many others harboured exactly that expectation. 'I have now upped my degree of difficulty by a very significant amount – that is one of the things that you have to take into account,' he said. 'At the moment everyone is probably expecting me to be up and nailing every single dive but it doesn't work like that. I'm the only diver in the world that has learned four new dives and put them straight into my list.'

Having attempted to manage public expectations, Tom then vowed to make the best efforts he could for further success. 'Normally people ease them in one by one,' he said of the new dives. 'I've gone and done all four in one year which is quite a tough ask. But I will continue to try and do my best.' The two-day meeting was broadcast live on the BBC Red Button, and also online on the BBC website, after the corporation had won the rights to broadcast swimming and aquatic sports coverage the previous month in a four-year deal.

Those who followed the action either in the pool

itself, or via the BBC's coverage, were in for a treat. Tom and Waterfield left it late to snatch in the 10-metre synchronized final, but they finished on top and claimed a gold medal. Nobody was more surprised than the duo themselves. In only their second international competition as a partnership, they had quite literally struck gold. The sell-out home crowd at Ponds Forge included a contingent of Tom fans – the Daley army that he had so hoped for. It was the four-and-a-half somersaults dive that had been a focus of their anxieties ahead of the event, yet on the day they performed it brilliantly. 'This is the dive that will make, or break, their chance of a medal,' explained the commentator as the tension built. 'Tom has really moved up to the big boys' league with a dive like this.' Tom stretched his legs on the platform, adjusted his trunks and prepared to jump, alongside Waterfield.

They pulled the dive off well, and as they hit the water the crowd celebrated loudly. Even the commentator joined in with unashamed patriotic fervour. 'Yeeessss!' he cried. 'Come on! Amazing! Amazing!'

Their marking was 365.55, which left them marginally behind their American rivals. Their final dive was the back two-and-a-half somersaults and two-and-a-half twists dive. 'Ready?' asked Waterfield at the top. 'Yeah,' said Tom. Waterfield counted them in for the jump: 'One, two, three . . . go,' and off they jumped.

It was an exceptional dive from the dynamic duo. As the commentator said, they were 'taking it to the Chinese' and their scoring for the final dive left them above their rivals. With 449.43, they beat the Chinese pairing of Cao Yuan and Zhang Yanquan who finished with 443.82.

Wonderful, rousing stuff. 'It's absolutely incredible, not at any point did we think we were going to win that,' said Tom afterwards. Speaking with unprecedented confidence and ebullience, he spoke of how they defeated their main opponents. 'The Chinese don't lose, especially with those two young Chinese divers, who when you come up against them most people say silver is gold,' he said. 'We just went out there and did our best; if you put the Chinese under pressure they don't like it.'

This was the bold, psychological chatter of a winner. Tom's competitive vigour was on show. His partner was no less jubilant, and the diving community was also hugely encouraged. The partnership on which so many hopes were resting was getting better by the day. 'That [the penultimate dive] was our newest dive and it saved us today,' said Waterfield of the four-and-a-half somersaults dive. Re-affirming that they had not been expecting to be among the medals, let alone at the top of the podium, he added: 'We wanted to come here and put in a good performance and if we got a medal it was a bonus – to get a gold medal is amazing.'

When it came to the 10-metre individual dive on the Saturday, Tom was not so lucky. There was a concern that the euphoria of the Friday night might lead to a less than positive performance on the Saturday. Tom watched Waterfield as his poor showing meant he missed out on a place in the final himself. Tom went into the final two dives of his qualifying round in last place – and he also looked set to miss the final. However, in his final two dives, Tom turned his fortunes round dramatically. The back three-and-a-half somersaults dive was a new and challenging hurdle for Tom, but he pulled it off with near perfection.

Finally, came a favourite of his, the reverse three-and-a-half somersaults. He again did well and, against many expectations, he snatched second place behind reigning World Series champion Qui Bo. 'There was some good stuff in there and some bad stuff as well,' Tom said. He had performed his first two dives well, and looked on course to be a contender for a medal. The Chinese contingent was on form but this time it was them putting Tom under pressure. Qui Bo and Liang Huo were close to perfection, and when Tom fluffed his armstand back triple somersaults dive, he was not to be among the medals. The dive had been doomed from the start, when he leaned too far away from the diving board. He then pushed himself too far away, and let go of his feet too late. He finished fourth.

'It was really annoying, actually,' said Tom looking back. He insisted he had got the 'best start' to the dive he had ever managed. So high had his spring been, he said, that he did not know how to react and salvage the dive. 'All the other dives were good,' he said with an air of slight defiance. There was no hiding that he was in less confident mood than he had been the last time he had spoken to the media. 'The way the Chinese are diving they are so far ahead of everyone at the moment, they are almost like machines, they are definitely the ones to watch ahead of London 2012,' he said. He watched as the winner of the 10-metre dive, Qui Bo, who had amassed a score of 586.55, took the gold. The man from China was on a run: this was his third World Series title in a row.

As for Tom, he reflected as best he could on the positives. His tactic of encouraging his growing fan-base to turn up at the event had paid dividends. The venue was sold out, and among the packed seating were plenty of fans who were there just to see Tom. As far as he was concerned, he hoped this would happen again and again. 'It's a great experience to have everyone supporting me here, it's a sell-out crowd, and I hope it will be the same in London. It really lifts you and makes you dive to the best of your ability,' he said.

Perhaps the more significant positive was that after he had ruined his armstand back triple somersaults dive he had still performed his next dive to perfection. Although it was too late at that stage to get back in medal contention, he still made the next one count. 'You can't ever let anything stop you in a competition,' he said. 'You just have to keep fighting and keep fighting until the end.'

He repeated his newfound admiration of the Chinese, perhaps evidence that he had regretted his previous fighting talk. Having won all four gold medals on day two, his admiration was understandable. 'The new dives are coming on, I just have to keep working hard and try my best and put as much pressure on the Chinese as I can because they are so far ahead of everyone else at the moment,' he said. 'Obviously I am disappointed with one of my dives but I have just got to make sure I can try to improve and focus for my next competition in Mexico,' he told the swimming. org website. 'My new dives are going quite well at the moment. I scored 9.5s for my back three-and-a-half which is the best that I have done internationally. Overall I am really pleased with this weekend. My dives were a bit inconsistent in Moscow and Beijing so to come here and do so well has given me a bit of confidence for this season.'

It had been an emotional weekend, not least due to Rob's presence in the audience. As he fought his latest brain tumour, he would have been more than justified to stay at home. Instead, he made a 600-mile round trip from Devon to Yorkshire, to cheer Tom on. He broke down in tears as the emotions and pressures he was facing bubbled up inside him, and his son deeply appreciated his father's effort. 'It was great to see him,' Tom told the *Daily Mail*. 'It was a bit emotional. He was upset because none of us knew for sure whether he would be able to get here. He did, and seeing him inspired me. His T-shirt had the words, "keep oil in my lamp, keep me burning", and he says that I am his oil. I think he'll be burning OK tonight.'

Tom spent a day with his family in Sheffield after the tournament had finished. They wanted to spend time together before Tom flew off to Mexico. He Tweeted an upbeat assessment of the second day in Sheffield, telling his 60,000+ followers: 'Ended up in 4th place today :(missed one of my dives but I wasn't far off the medals considering how badly I missed the dive! Positive :)'

Meanwhile, Andy Banks said that Tom had every reason to be proud of his performance in Sheffield. 'I don't want to get carried away but in the synchro, I think I'm right in saying that's the first time the Chinese have been beaten in a World Series final,' he said. He also pointed out that Tom's placement in the finals of the individual dives, and Waterfield's absence from them, saw a role reversal from Beijing. 'Encouragingly, Tom's difficult dive tariffs, which he's been working on, has become more consistent,' Banks said.

The closing message of the Sheffield event came in the form, as ever, of a look ahead to 2012. Tom and Waterfield both agreed that their best chance of a gold medal in the Olympics would lie in the 10-metre synchro event.

Tom's stay in Guanajuato, Mexico, for the FINA Diving World Series was not to be a particularly happy time. He arrived tired, after a long flight that had required an early start. On his arrival, he Tweeted to his followers that he was looking forward to some sleep; but the following day, he took to Twitter again, telling them that he was 'knackered' after his first day's training. Later that day his mood was not improved when a passing bird fouled him. 'Great! Haha,' he said on Twitter. Sadly, that incident did not even bring with it the fabled good luck that is said to follow. Tom and Waterfield did not repeat their dynamics of Sheffield in the synchro round. 'Not a great competition :/ 5th overall :(' said Tom on Twitter. Their 402.75 score had left them in fifth place. The star partnership of the event had been the home duo of Ivan Garcia and

German Sanchez, who took gold.

Fatigue, bird poo and a disappointing performance when it mattered – it certainly had not been a good start. He could only learn from the setback in the pool and hope to bounce back in the individual rounds the following day.

He did. Finishing second in the preliminary round, Tom got his highest score of 2011. In the final he finished second and took silver. Proudly announcing this on Twitter, he told his devoted followers: 'I got a 10 on front 4.5 and a personal best and British record :) wooop!' His overall total had been 562.80, with Waterfield trailing outside the medals in fifth place, with a score of just 512. A decent ending to the series then, for Tom at least.

While there was concern over his and Waterfield's partnership in Mexico, in the individual round Tom's fine scoring was the source of much pleasure. In the wake of the event, Tom moved on to Guadalajara for some outdoor training. As he hit the road, he was cheered from a Tweet from Waterfield, who wrote: 'Well didn't dive great again hit 3 missed 3 & came 5, but @TomDaley1994 dived sick!!! Well done mate!'

CHAPTER TWELVE

•

Doing it for Rob

'If I could be half the dad that my dad was to me then that would be my best achievement.'

TOM DALEY

DIVING WAS VERY MUCH IN NEED of the boost that Tom's popularity has given it. In recent years there has been a decline in both the number of swimming pools open, and the number of pools including diving facilities. In 1977 there were 296 diving facilities for the public; by 2008 this number had dropped to just sixty-six. Nowhere is this trend more keenly felt than in London. In the capital in 1977 there were ninety-six pools with diving facilities and by 2008 there were just six: a massive loss of 96 per cent.

This drift left eight British counties with no diving facilities at all, including all of Norfolk and Suffolk. It does not take a genius to work out that there is little chance of a new Tom Daley emerging from those counties. Many pools have been closed to make way for new housing developments. Despite swimming being one of Britain's most popular sporting activities – with around 50 per cent of British schoolchildren regularly taking part. The closures continue on one hand, while childhood obesity continues to rise on the other.

As more pools close, swimming organizations have campaigned hard against closure, with one group describing the situation as nothing less than a 'national disaster'. When a pool closed in Blaenavon, in Wales, locals were so angry that they held a mock 'funeral' protest. Wales has become a particularly striking example of this problem. As of 2011, it has no usable high-board.

The National Curriculum has had its own destructive effect. Its demand for increased classroom space in schools has led to many establishments knocking down their pools to build new classrooms. A damning Ofsted report concluded that for twenty-first-century schools there is: 'too little time for swimming; staff unable to get children to overcome fear of water in available time; inappropriate curriculum; poor leadership and management.'

Diving pools have extra costs, including additional heating and lifeguard expenditure. However, a more global problem has also been to blame. FINA, the worldwide diving authority, issued a ruling that all diving pools must have a minimum depth of thirteen feet. Excruciatingly, many British pools were just inches too shallow to meet this ruling.

It is ironic that this decline in facilities has coincided with that upsurge in interest in diving and swimming, largely due to the success and general appeal of Tom Daley. He is all too aware of this irony and of the obstacles it puts in the way of those who might wish to follow in his footsteps. 'There isn't enough access for people across the country,' he said. 'There could be another British diving world champion out there but if they don't have facilities nearby they might never discover their talent.'

On a more positive note, some diving experts claim that many of the facilities that have closed were of poor quality and are therefore of little loss to the sport. Furthermore, the number of people enrolled with diving clubs has increased ten-fold over the past thirty years. In the last ten years, the number of diving coaches has doubled. This renewed passion can be seen in the increasingly lengthy queues at Britain's diving pools, such as those at Guildford and Southampton.

In the run-up to London 2012, the broadcasting authorities have sensed this newfound interest in diving and swimming and have begun to transmit more of it, with the BBC, in particular, showing more diving and swimming competitions of late, including the FINA World Series event in Sheffield April 2011. This is a trend for which Tom is proudly a significant, leading catalyst.

Rarely have water sports been more popular.

Although it is grossly premature to speak of the legacy left by someone who is still only in his teens, if Tom's legacy was to have reignited a nation's interest in physical activity and fitness, it will be a worthwhile one to say the least.

As far back as 2000, the Medical Research Council wrote to MPs warning that fifty per cent of British adults were overweight, and one in five were obese. To illustrate the problem, obesity levels in Britain were compared to those in France, where just one in ten adults was found to be obese. By 2008, the problem had not improved and experts were warning it would become worse. Using the 2012 Olympics as a signpost to aim towards, researchers claimed that by the time the tournament came round that one-third of Brits would be obese.

With a large percentage of obese people coming from low-income families, swimming and other water sports become positive options for this trend to be tackled. It is a low-cost activity, and unlike gym use, it can be paid for on a per-visit basis rather than requiring deposits and monthly payments. Also, children can learn to swim and develop a passion for it at school – but only if they have the resources. Tom feels strongly that these opportunities should remain for children, and in December 2010 he added his name to a letter that questioned the wisdom of the cutting of the £162m ring-fenced fund for partnerships between schools. 'With one ill-conceived cut you are on the brink of destroying everything schools, clubs and the national governing bodies of sport are doing to ensure this and future generations embrace sport and physical activity, not shun it,' said the letter. Among the other signatories were cyclist Jamie Staff, boxer James DeGale, and sailor Andrew Simpson. In these times of 'austerity', sporting bodies must keep their eye on the cuts in order to ensure a new generation of fine British athletes emerge.

Meanwhile, his popularity as a teenage heartthrob shows no sign of abating. His Twitter following is growing by the day. If he continues to use the social networking website wisely, he can easily build his popularity. A random examination of Tweets written by his fans, either to or about him, show that for many the details of his sport are of little interest beyond the fact that diving means they see him wearing just his speedos a lot of the time.

'Tom Daley? Just marry me. Right now,' reads one Tweet from a teenage girl. 'Oh Tom Daley you beaut,' writes another. A different fan sent a jokingly angry rebuke to a friend who had expressed admiration of him. 'Btw, tom daley is MINE. You said you didn't like him?' The fact that Tom is clearly the topic of family conversations comes across in several messages. 'The awkward moment when your mum tells your uncle about your undying love for Tom Daley . . .' writes one fan. Another recounts with an air of mischief: 'hahaha dad keeps moaning at me cos me and mum made him watch tom daley videos earlier')' However, many of the mentions of Tom are of more of the 'teen hysteria' variety. The message: 'SOMEONE JUST MENTIONED TOM DALEY ON TV OH MY GOD I'M GOING TO DIE <3333333333', is of a typical tone.

The above Tweets are just a snapshot of those written about Tom during a twenty-four hour period in April 2011. They are a representative selection, as subsequent searches confirmed. Perhaps most significant of all is that the twenty-four hour period in question was one in which Tom was involved in a very important diving competition – the final leg of the World Series in Mexico. True, there were some messages about him on Twitter that acknowledged this fact. However, it is surprising and noteworthy that a majority of those who were Tweeting admiringly of him that weekend seemed unaware that he was involved in a crucial dive meeting.

This shows the nature of Tom's fame: thanks to his good looks, teenage appeal and easy way with the media, a significant proportion of those who know and admire him care little for the nuts and bolts of his profession. This is not an entirely peculiar state of affairs for a pin-up sportsman. It is easy to suppose that some of those girls who fancied David Beckham during the prime of his career were unaware of the day-to-day details of his football commitments. However, given the prominence of football in the twenty-first century, this proportion would have been relatively low. In Tom's case, with diving a far less popular sport, the truth is that many of those girls who adore him are not interested in his career.

In time, this might change. As we have seen, diving is noticeably growing in media stature and general popularity thanks to Tom's involvement. Also, if he continues to pursue opportunities to make more general media appearances, and particularly if he one day realizes his dream of becoming a fully fledged television presenter, the details of his life will be more accessible to his fan-base. Though he stands in a strange place as a celebrity, this is a positive thing for him. It shows what a magnetic and adorable character he is in the eyes of his fans that they are so enamoured by him in spite of, rather than because of, the career that made him famous.

Even Blake Aldridge wishes Tom nothing but the best. Despite their differences and the abrupt ending to their partnership, Aldridge is full of admiration and good wishes for Tom. 'I wish him well whoever he dives with in synchro, and individually,' he told me. 'Tom's been fantastic for British diving – for everybody involved. He's carried himself in a very mature way throughout his career. I think if he does well in 2012 he's going to help British diving. He's making it good for the kids coming through. If Tom does well, it keeps the funding up. That gives younger kids a chance, and that is more important than anything else.'

Meanwhile, 'England expects' ahead of 2012. So entwined with that tournament has the narrative of Tom's professional life been, that the expectation and hope surrounding him has risen ever higher with each passing month. So much is different now, as Olympic medallist Leon Taylor succinctly explained. 'When Tom was in Beijing, he was just fourteen,' said Taylor. 'No one apart from the media expected him to medal, so the hype got ahead of him, which often happens. This time around, Tom has been world champion at just fifteen in 2009, double Commonwealth champion last year and has had a fantastic year so far.'

•

One of Tom's favourite songs is *Peaceful Easy Feeling*, by The Eagles. 'This song means a lot to me because it was the song that my dad used to sing to me when I was going to sleep as a baby,' he said. 'He tells me that every time he hears the song, and he always plays it when we are in the car.' The song speaks of a peaceful, easy feeling, and a faith that the vocalist will not be let down.

Rob had often sung the song at karaoke bars – and

Tom himself even sang it once. It was at one of the family's annual 'Rob's still here' parties, thrown to celebrate Rob's defiance of cancer. The disease finally claimed his life on 27 May 2011. Tom and the other members of the immediate family were at Rob's bedside as he slipped away. In the final hours, Tom had written of his love for his father on his Twitter page. 'I love you so much Dad,' he wrote.

The news was broken to the world in a statement from British Swimming. It read: 'Tom Daley's father, Rob Daley, lost his battle with cancer yesterday 27 May at 21.35 hours. He passed away peacefully with his family at his side. His health has been fluctuating since February but he continued to fight until the last day, defying doctors' expectations. The family have asked for respect to their privacy during this very difficult period.'

It was a testament to Rob's personality and the part he had played in Tom's success that news of his death was met with upset and grief on the part of many people in Britain who had never met him.

In the days that followed Rob's death, Tom paid tribute to him on Twitter. Within hours of his father's death, he wrote: 'If I could be half the dad that my dad was to me then that would be my best achievement! I love you! Xx'. A few hours later he thanked his followers and fans for all the well-wishing messages they had sent. Then, he made an affectionate reference to Rob's eccentricity, Tweeting: '"give me oil in my lamp keep me burning" my dad had a funny outlook on life!' It was both touching and heart-breaking, to see how bravely young Tom appeared to be responding to the death of his beloved father.

Rob's funeral took place in early June at St Mary's Church in Plympton, Plymouth. Tom gave a eulogy at the private service, attended by 200 people. Among the hymns, the mourners sang *Jerusalem* and also listened to one of Rob's favourite songs, *Unchained Melody*. Then they sang the hymn *Give Me Joy In My Heart* – the hymn that had inspired Rob's famous T-shirt slogan. There were few dry eyes.

Afterwards, Tom released a statement. 'My dad was an incredibly brave man, completely dedicated to his family, with a love for all,' it read. He also vowed that he would make his father and nation proud of him. Although Tom was already determined to make a success of his diving and to win gold at London 2012, the death of his father only made that resolve more steely and focused. In the countdown to the tournament, he would allow nothing to distract him from his goal.

•

However, in July he came home without a medal from the World Championships in Shanghai. He had watched with amazement as China's Qiu Bo won the individual platform event. Bo had been on unbeatable form: managing three perfect 10s. On his return to Britain, Tom announced that he would be quitting school to focus on his preparations for the Olympics. 'From January onwards I'm going to take a break from school, so that I have that half a year to train for the Olympics,' he said. 'I'm hoping to get my A-levels done by then and if I have to retake any of them I'll do that in June or go back to school the following year. It's going to be good to concentrate on diving rather than splitting my time with school. I've never done that before. I will be able to work on my consistency, with nothing else to worry about. It's important when you are diving against the Chinese. They are so far ahead of everyone else.'

At the London Olympics in 2012, Tom will have the home support firmly on his side. The British public's respect and affection for him has only deepened since his family's bereavement. At just seventeen, he is firmly established as a national hero with a place in the hearts of millions.

When he treads onto the gleaming Olympic diving boards at the wonderful new Aquatics Centre – at the opening of which Tom performed the inaugural dive – in August 2012, the nation will be rooting for him. Whatever happens there, he has already achieved enough in his short life to make any father proud.

TOM DALEY'S
MAJOR DIVING HONOURS

Gold medal at British Championships, 2004

Gold medal at Australian Junior Elite Diving
Championships, 2005

Silver medal winner, ASA National Championships, 2006

Double gold medal winner, ASA National
Championships, 2007

Silver in synchronized diving at Australian Youth Olympic
Festival, 2007

Gold and silver medal winner, British Championships,
2007

Double gold medal winner, British Championships, 2008

Gold medal winner, British Championships, 2009

Gold medal winner, European Championships, 2008

Bronze medal winner, FINA Diving World Cup, 2008

Gold, silver and bronze medal winner, FINA Diving World
Series, 2009

Grand Prix winner, 2009

Commonwealth gold medal-winner in 10-metre platform and synchro, 2010

Silver medal-winner, British Gas National Cup, 2010

Silver medal-winner, British Gas National Cup, 2011

Other significant honours

Youngster of the Year, BBC South West, 2005

BBC Young Sports Personality of the Year, 2007, 2009 and 2010

Listed at number 63 in *Time* magazine's '100 Olympic Athletes to Watch', 2008

South West Sports Personality of the Year 2009

Short-listed to final 10 for the BBC Sports Personality of the Year award in 2009 and 2010

ACKNOWLEDGEMENTS

With thanks to Louise Dixon and Michael O'Mara. I am also grateful to everyone who helped me research this book, including those who preferred to not be named. Thanks to Blake Aldridge and Richard Lenton for the fascinating interviews, and also to Chris Morris, Peregrine Dixon and Jonathan Sacerdoti for their help and encouragement.

I am thankful to all who have bought any of my books, and to those readers from around the world who have taken the trouble to write encouraging letters, emails and 'tweets'. Particular gratitude in that regard goes to Alanah and Nikki Mudie – 'Shawty' still sits on my desk and inspires me.

PICTURE

ACKNOWLEDGEMENTS

Page 1: Mirrorpix (above left); Richard Lappas/Rex Features (above right); Robert Hallam/Rex Features (below)

Page 2: Adrian Sherratt/Rex Features (above); South West News Service/Rex Features (below left and right)

Page 3: Phil Walter/Getty Images (above); Matt Roberts/Rex Features (below)

Page 4: Andy Hooper/Associated Newspapers/Rex Features (both)

Page 5: Tim Graham/Getty Images (above); David Fisher/Rex Features (below)

Page 6: AGF s.r.l./Rex Features (above left); Olycom SPA/Rex Features (above right); Barry Gomer/Rex Features (below)

Page 7: Back Page Images/Rex Features (above); Stefan Rousseau/WPA Pool/Getty Images (below left); David Dyson, Camera Press London (below right)

Page 8: Rex Features (above); Clive Rose/Getty Images (below left and right)

INDEX